KU-167-378

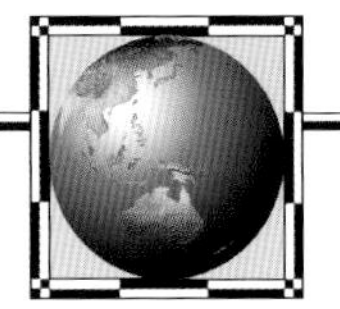

WORLD ATLAS

David Ross

First published in the UK in 1999 by
Caxton Editions
16 Connaught Street
Marble Arch
London W2 2AF

ISBN: 1-84067-092-4

This is a MARS book

Edited, designed and produced by Haldane Mason, London

Acknowledgements

Art Director: Ron Samuels

Editorial Director: Sydney Francis

Editor: Jane Ellis

Design: Zoë Mellors

Printed in China

Contents

Countries of the World

Country Official designation	Capital Population	Population	Area In sq km	Language * = official language	Flag
AFRICA					
Algeria Democratic Republic of Algeria	Algiers 1,700,000	25,878,000	2,381,741	*Arabic Berber	
Angola Republic of Angola	Luanda 1,130,00	10,548,000	1,266,700	*Portuguese Bantu	
Benin Republic of Benin	Porto Novo 170,000	5,900,000	112,622	*French Fon, Yoruba	
Botswana Republic of Botswana	Gaborone 134,000	1,600,000	600,372	*English Tswana	
Burkina-Faso Republic of Burkina-Faso	Ouagadougou 459,000	9,755,000	274,200	*French Fulani	
Burundi Republic of Burundi	Bujumbura 236,000	6,050,000	27,834	*French *Rundi	
Cameroon Republic of Cameroon	Yaoundé 653,700	12,183,000	475,442	*French *English	
Cape Verde Republic of Cape Verde	Praia 62,300	393,000	4,033	*Portuguese Crioulu	
Central African Republic	Bangui 600,000	3,344,000	622,436	*French Sangho	
Chad Republic of Chad	N'djamena 598,000	7,166,000	1,285,000	*Arabic *French	
Comoros Republic of the Comoros	Moroni 22,000	494,000	1,862	*Arabic *French	
Congo People's Republic of the Congo	Brazzaville 770,000	2,583,000	342,000	*French	
Djibouti Republic of Djibouti	Djibouti 222,000	454,000	23,200	*Arabic *French	
Egypt Arab Republic of Egypt	Cairo 6,200,000	54,879,000	942,247	*Arabic	

Equatorial Guinea Republic of Equatorial Guinea	Malabu 31,000	350,000	28,051	*Spanish Bubi
Eritrea	Asmara 333,000	3,683,000	121,143	*Tigrinya *Arabic
Ethiopia	Addis Ababa 1,704,000	51,064,000	1,130,139	*Amharic Arabic
Gabon Gabonese Republic	Libreville 352,000	1,256,000	267,667	*French Bantu
Gambia Republic of the Gambia	Banjul 44,800	1,261,000	11,295	*English
Ghana Republic of Ghana	Accra 987,000	15,796,000	238,538	*English Akan
Guinea: Republic of Guinea	Conakry 707,000	7,509,000	254,857	*French
Guinea-Bissau Republic of Guinea-Bissau	Bissau 126,000	1, 237,000	36,125	*Portuguese Creole
Ivory Coast Republic of the Ivory Coast	Yamoussoukro 123,000	15,010,000	322,463	*French
Kenya Republic of Kenya	Nairobi 1,485,000	23,425,000	582,646	*Swahili Kikuyu, English
Lesotho Kingdom of Lesotho	Maseru 112,300	1,917,000	30,355	*English Sesotho
Liberia Republic of Liberia	Monrovia 465,000	2,759,000	111,369	*English
Libya Arab Republic of Libya	Tripoli 593,000	5,874,000	1,775,500	*Arabic
Madagascar Democratic Republic of Madagascar	Tananarive 1,100,000	14,376,000	587,041	Malagasy French
Malawi Republic of Malawi	Lilongwe 220,000	9,702,000	118,484	*English Nyanja
Mali Republic of Mali	Bamako 650,000	9,854,000	1,240,142	*French Bambara
Mauritania: Islamic Republic of Mauritania	Nouakchott 397,000	2,3467,000	1,030,700	*Arabic

Mauritius Republic of Mauritius	Port Louis 145,000	1,134,000	2,045	*English Creole, French
Morocco Kingdom of Morocco	Rabat 556,000	25,878,000	458,730	*Arabic Berber
Mozambique Republic of Mozambique	Maputo 987,000	18,165,000	799,380	*Portuguese
Namibia Republic of Namibia	Windhoek 115,000	1,799,000	824,292	*Afrikaans English
Niger Republic of Niger	Niamey 410,000	8,005,000	1,186,408	*French Hausa
Nigeria Federal Republic of Nigeria	Abuja 379,000	88,760,000	923,768	*English Hausa, Ibo, Yoruba
Rwanda Rwandese Republic	Kigali 236,000	6,903,000	26,338	Kinyarwanda French
Sao Tomé & Principe Democratic Republic of Sao Tomé & Principe	Sao Tomé 35,000	130,00	964	*Portuguese
Senegal Republic of Senegal	Dakar 1,503,000	9,502,000	196,722	*French Wolof
Seychelles Republic of Seychelles	Victoria 24,900	70,000	453	*Creole English
Sierra Leone Republic of Sierra Leone	Freetown 490,000	4,954,000	71,740	*English Krio
Somalia Somali Democratic Republic	Mogadishu 550,000	6,570,000	637,657	*Somali Arabic
South Africa Republic of South Africa	Pretoria 447,000 Cape Town 900,000	38,354,000	1,224,641	*Afrikaans *English
Sudan Republic of Sudan	Khartoum 561,000	25,000,000	2,505,813	*Arabic
Swaziland Kingdom of Swaziland	Mbabane 38,000	1,132,000	17,364	*English *Swazi
Tanzania Republic of Tanzania	Dodoma 210,000	26,620,000	939,470	Swahili, English

Togo Togolese Republic	Lomé 405,000	4,867,000	56,785	*French Ewe, Hausa 
Tunisia Republic of Tunisia	Tunis 630,000	9,521,000	163,610	*Arabic 
Uganda Republic of Uganda	Kampala 655,000	17,144,000	241,038	*Swahili *English 
Zaire Republic of Zaire	Kinshasa 3,800,000	36,859,000	2,344,885	*French 
Zambia Republic of Zambia	Lusaka 987,000	8,237,000	752,614	*English 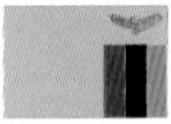
Zimbabwe Republic of Zimbabwe	Harare 869,000	11,585,000	390,759	*English 

NORTH AMERICA AND CENTRAL AMERICA

Antigua and Barbuda	St John's 36,000	66,000	442	*English Creole 
Bahamas Commonwealth of the Bahamas	Nassau 172,000	263,000	13,939	*English Creole 
Barbados	Bridgetown 8,000	261,000	431	English 
Belize	Belmopan 3,900	190,000	22,965	*English Creole, Spanish 
Canada	Ottawa 303,000	27, 380,000	9,970,610	English, French 
Costa Rica Republic of Costa Rica	San José 297,000	3,534,000	51,100	Spanish 
Cuba Republic of Cuba	Havana 2,130,000	10,999,000	110,922	Spanish 
Dominica Commonwealth of Dominica	Roseau 16,000	67,000	751	*English 
Dominican Republic	Santo Domingo 1,600,000	7,910,000	48,442	*Spanish 
El Salvador Republic of El Salvador	San Salvador 482,000	5,661,000	21,041	Spanish, Maya Nahua 

Country	Capital / Population	Population	Area	Languages
Grenada State of Grenada	Saint George's 7,500	87,000	344	*English Creole
Guatemala Republic of Guatemala	Guatemala City 1,120,000	11,600,000	108,889	*Spanish Maya
Haiti Republic of Haiti	Port-au-Prince 515,000	6,614,000	27,400	Creole, French
Honduras Republic of Honduras	Tegucigalpa 608,000	4,990,000	112,088	*Spanish Maya
Jamaica	Kingston 110,000	2,614,000	10,991	English
Mexico United States of Mexico	Mexico City 8,500,000	82,880,00	1,972,547	*Spanish Nahua, Maya
Nicaragua Republic of Nicaragua	Managua 690,000	4,127,000	130,682	*Spanish
Panama Republic of Panama	Panama City 412,000	2,694,000	77,082	*Spanish
St Christopher & Nevis Federation of St Christopher & Nevis	Basseterre 20,000	46,000	269	*English Creole
St Lucia	Castries 52,000	156,000	616	*English Creole
St Vincent & The Grenadines	Kingstown 26,900	111,000	389	*English Creole
United States United States of America	Washington 610,000	253,084,000	9,355,855	English

SOUTH AMERICA

Country	Capital / Population	Population	Area	Languages
Argentina Argentine Republic	Buenos Aires 3,101,000	33,323,000	2,780,092	*Spanish Tupi, Quechua
Bolivia Republic of Bolivia	La Paz (admin.) 126,000 Sucre (legal) 105,000	7,872,000	1,098,581	Spanish Quechua
Brazil Republic of Brazil	Brasilia 1,600,000	147,440,000	8,511,996	*Portuguese Carib, Tupi

Country	Capital / Population	Population	Area	Languages
Chile Republic of Chile	Santiago 5,200,00	13,514,000	756,626	*Spanish Araucanian
Colombia Republic of Colombia	Santa Fe de Bogotà 5,000,000	33,808,000	1,141,748	*Spanish
Ecuador Republic of Ecuador	Quito 1,120,000	10,000,000	283,561	*Spanish Quechua
Guyana Cooperative Republic of Guyana	Georgetown 200,000	771,000	214,970	*English Creole, Hindi
Paraguay Republic of Paraguay	Asunción 612,000	4,328,000	406,752	*Spanish Tupi
Peru Republic of Peru	Lima 6,250,000	22,152,000	1,285,216	*Spanish *Quechua *Aymara
Suriname Republic of Suriname	Paramaribo 68,000	433,000	163,820	*Dutch Carib, Creole
Trinidad and Tobago Republic of Trinidad & Tobago	Port of Spain 62,000	1,279,000	5,123	*English Hindu
Uruguay Eastern Republic of Uruguay	Montevideo 1,269,000	3,198,000	176,215	Spanish
Venezuela Republic of Venezuela	Caracas 1,311,00	19,899,000	912,050	*Spanish Carib

ASIA AND THE MIDDLE EAST

Country	Capital / Population	Population	Area	Languages
Afghanistan Republic of Afghanistan	Kabul 1,400,000	16,900,000	652,225	Dari, Pashto
Armenia Armenian Republic	Yerevan 1,215,000	3,330,000	29,800	Armenian
Azerbaijan Republic of Azerbaijan	Baku 1,150,000	7,199,000	86,600	Azerbaijani
Bahrain State of Bahrain	Manama 150,000	518,000	678	Arabic
Bangladesh People's Republic of Bangladesh	Dhaka 6,290,000	105,500,000	143,998	*Bengali English
Belarus Republic of Belarus	Minsk 1,600,000	10,367,000	207,600	Belarussian

Bhutan Realm of the Dragon	Thimphu 30,000	1,494,000	47,000	Dzongkha 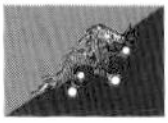
Brunei Darussalam Sultanate of Brunei	Bandar Seri Begawan 56,000	266,000	5,765	Malay, English 
Cambodia State of Kampuchea	Phnomh Penh 564,000	8,830,000	181,035	*Khmer French 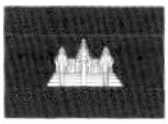
China People's Republic of China	Beijing 7,362,000	1,190,000,000	9,536,499	Chinese 
Cyprus Republic of Cyprus	Nicosia 190,000	719,000	9,251	Greek Turkish
Georgia Republic of Georgia	Tbilisi 1,260,000	5,551,000	69,700	Georgian 
Kazakhstan Kazakh Republic	Alma-Ata 1,130,000	16,838,000	2,717,300	Kazakh 
Kyrgyzstan Kyrgyz Republic	Bishkek 625,000	4,462,000	198,500	Kirghiz 
India Republic of India	Delhi 300,000	851,600,000	3,287,782	*Hindi, English Bengali, Urdu 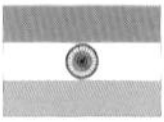
Indonesia Republic of Indonesia	Jakarta 9,160,000	181,100,000	1,529,072	*Bahasa Indonesia 
Iran Islamic Republic of Iran	Tehran 6,600,000	56,301,000	1,648,196	Farsi 
Iraq Republic of Iraq	Baghdad 3,900,000	17,950,000	434,128	Arabic Kurdish 
Israel State of Israel	Jerusalem 530,000	4,975,000	20,700	*Hebrew Arabic 
Japan Nippon	Tokyo 8,200,000	124,180,000	372,819	Japanese
Jordan Hashemite Kin gdom of Jordan	Amman 980,000	3,344,000	97,740	Arabic 
Kuwait State of Kuwait	Kuwait City 45,000	2,241,000	17,818	Arabic 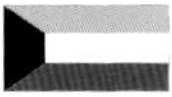
Laos Lao People's Democratic Republic	Vientiane 380,000	4,322,000	236,800	*Lao French 

Country	Capital / Population	Population	Area	Languages
Lebanon Republic of Lebanon	Beirut 490,000	2,950,000	10,400	Arabic French
Malaysia Federation of Malaysia	Kuala Lumpur 1,103,000	18,400,000	329,758	*Malay, English, Chinese
Maldives Republic of Maldives	Malé 56,000	230,000	298	Maldivian
Moldova Moldovan Republic	Chisinau 665,000	4,457,000	33,700	Romanian
Mongolia Mongolian Republic	Ulan Bator 550,000	2,350,000	1,566,500	Khalka
Myanmar Union of Myanmar	Rangoon 2,505,000	42,560,000	678,033	*Burmese English
Nepal Kingdom of Nepal	Kathmandu 401,000	19,412,000	147,181	*Nepali Bihari
North Korea Democratic People's Republic of Korea	Pyongyang 2,639,000	22,900,000	120,538	Korean
Oman Sultanate of Oman	Muscat 50,000	1,579,000	212,457	*Arabic
Pakistan Islamic Republic of Pakistan	Islamabad 210,000	115,740,000	796,095	Urdu, English
Philippines Republic of the Philippines	Manila 1,620,000	62,240,000	300,000	Pilipino, English
Qatar State of Qatar	Doha 220,000	467,000	11,437	Arabic
Russia Federal Republic of Russia	Moscow 8,769,000	150,100,000	17,075,400	Russian
Saudi Arabia Kingdom of Saudi Arabia	Riyadh 1,312,000	15,294,000	2,153,168	Arabic
Singapore Republic of Singapore	Singapore 2,987,000	2,987,000	639	Chinese Malay, English
South Korea Republic of South Korea	Seoul 10,915,000	43,730,000	99,237	*Korean
Sri Lanka Democratic Socialist Republic of Sri Lanka	Colombo 615,000	17,321,000	65,610	*Sinhalese *Tamil

Country	Capital / Population	Population	Area	Language
Syria Arabic Republic of Syria	Damascus 1,388,000	12,524,000	185,180	Arabic
Tajikistan Republic of Tajikistan	Dushanbe 595,000	5,512,000	143,100	Tadhzik
Taiwan Republic of China	Taipei 2,943,000	20,489,000	36,202	Chinese
Thailand Kingdom of Thailand	Bangkok 5,982,000	55,966,000	513,115	Thai
Turkey Republic of Turkey	Ankara 2,559,000	51,385,000	755,688	*Turkish
Turkmenistan	Ashkabad 398,000	3,720,000	488,100	Turkmen
Ukraine	Kiev 2,587,000	51,988,000	603,700	Ukrainian
United Arab Emirates	Abu Dhabi 143,000	1,970,000	83,600	*Arabic
Uzbekistan Republic of Uzbekistan	Tashkent 2,070,000	20,731,000	447,400	Uzbek
Vietnam Socialist Republic of Vietnam	Hanoi 1,112,000	67,765,000	329,566	Vietnamese
Yemen Republic of Yemen	Sana' 427,000	11,853,000	524,342	Arabic

AUSTRALASIA AND THE PACIFIC

Country	Capital / Population	Population	Area	Language
Australia Commonwealth of Australia	Canberra 302,500	17,104,000	7,682,300	English
Fiji Republic of Fiji	Suva 70,000	739,000	18,272	Fijian, English
Kiribati Republic of Kiribati	Beiriki 2,200	72,000	849	*English
Marshall Islands Republic of the Marshall Islands	Majuro 30,000	60,000	181	*English Marshallese
Micronesia Federated States of Micronesia	Kolonia 5000	113,000	707	English

Nauru Republic of Nauru	Yaren 9,000	9,000	21	*Nauruan English 
New Zealand	Wellington 148,000	3,412,000	270,534	English Maori 
Palau	Koror 10,500	15,000	587	English Palauan
Papua New Guinea	Port Moresby 152,000	3,600,000	462,840	*English Tok Pisin 
Solomon Islands	Honiara 36,000	319,000	28,369	*English 
Tonga Kingdom of Tonga	Nuku'alofa 29,000	96,000	748	English Tongan 
Tuvalu The Tuvalu Islands	Fongafale 1000	9,000	24	Tuvaluan English 
Vanuatu Republic of Vanuatu	Port-Vila 20,000	148,000	12,189	*English *French 
Western Samoa Independent State of Western Samoa	Apia 34,500	164,000	2,831	*Samoan

EUROPE

Albania Republic of Albania	Tirana 243,000	3,230,00	28,748	*Albanian 
Andorra Principality of Andorra	Andorra-la-Vella 15,600	52,000	453	*Catalan 
Austria Republic of Austria	Vienna 1,806,000	7,780,000	83,859	German 
Belgium Kingdom of Belgium	Brussels 960,000	9,990,000	30,5188	Flemish, French 
Bosnia-Herzegovina Republic of Bosnia-Herzegovina	Sarajevo 537,000	4,350,000	51,129	Serbo-Croat
Bulgaria Republic of Bulgaria	Sofia 1,267,000	9,000,000	110,994	Bulgarian 
Croatia Republic of Croatia	Zagreb 868,000	4,802,000	51,129	Croat 

Country	Capital	Population	Area	Language
Czech Republic	Prague 1,234,000	10,387,000	78,864	Czech 
Denmark Kingdom of Denmark	Copenhagen 626,000	5,190,000	43,093	Danish 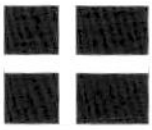
Estonia Republic of Estonia	Tallinn 489,000	1,580,000	45,100	Estonian 
Finland Republic of Finland	Helsinki 512,000	4,992,000	338,145	Finnish Swedish 
France French Republic	Paris 2,152,000	56,660,000	543,965	French
Germany Federal Republic of Germany	Berlin 3,470,000	79,501,000	356,957	German
Greece Hellenic Republic	Athens 894,000	10,193,000	131,957	Greek 
Hungary Hungarian Republic	Budapest 2,088,000	10,377,000	93,033	Hungarian (Magyar) 
Iceland Republic of Iceland	Reykjavik 97,000	255,000	102,819	Icelandic 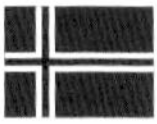
Ireland Republic of Ireland	Dublin 915,000	3,581,000	70,283	*Gaelic, English 
Italy Italian Republic	Rome 2,693,000	56,880,000	301,302	Italian 
Latvia	Riga 927,000	2,705,000	64,500	Latvian 
Liechtenstein Principality of Liechtenstein	Vaduz 5000	29,000	160	German 
Lithuania	Vilnius 591,000	3,756,000	65,200	Lithuanian 
Luxembourg Grand Duchy of Luxembourg	Luxembourg 78,000	383,000	2,586	French, German 
Macedonia Republic of Macedonia	Skopje 420,000	2,050,000	25,713	Macedonian 
Malta Republic of Malta	Valletta 9,800	355,000	316	Maltese English 

Monaco Principality of Monaco	Monaco 1,200	31,000	2	French 
Netherlands Kingdom of the Netherlands	Amsterdam 1,100,000	15,900,000	41,574	Dutch 
Norway Kingdom of Norway	Oslo 473,000	4,263,000	323,878	Norwegian 
Poland Republic of Poland	Warsaw 1,901,000	38,220,000	312,683	Polish
Portugal Portuguese Republic	Lisbon 874,000	10,350,000	91,191	Portuguese 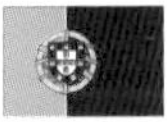
Romania	Bucharest 2,236,000	23,210,000	237,500	Romanian
San Marino Most Serene Republic of San Marino	San Marino 2,300	23,000	61	Italian
Slovakia Republic of Slovakia	Bratislava 441,000	5,303,000	49,036	Slovak 
Slovenia Republic of Slovenia	Ljubljana 267,000	1,970,000	20,251	Slovene 
Spain Kingdom of Spain	Madrid 2,976,000	37,011,000	498,507	Spanish 
Sweden Kingdom of Sweden	Stockholm 703,000	8,561,000	449,964	Swedish 
Switzerland Swiss Confederation	Berne 128,000	6,786,000	41,285	German, French, Italian, Rhaeto-Romansch 
United Kingdom United Kingdom of Great Britain and Northern Ireland	London 6,962,000	55,512,000	244,100	English 
Vatican City State of the Vatican City	Vatican City 1,000	1000	1	*Italian, *Latin 
Yugoslavia Federal Republic of Yugoslavia	Belgrade 1,136,000	10,360,000	102,173	Serbo-Croat 

1 Guyana
2 Suriname
3 French Guiana
4 Netherlands
5 Belgium
6 Luxembourg
7 Andorra
8 Switzerland
9 Austria
10 Germany
11 Estonia
12 Latvia
13 Lithuania
14 Russia
15 Poland
16 Czech Republic
17 Slovenia
18 Croatia
19 Bosnia-Herz.
20 Belarus
21 Slovak Republic
22 Hungary
23 Yugoslavia
24 Albania
25 Ukraine
26 Moldavia
27 Romania
28 Bulgaria
29 Macedonia
30 Greece
31 Cyprus
32 Lebanon
33 Israel
34 Qatar
35 United Arab Emirates
36 Burkina Faso
37 Ivory Coast
38 Ghana
39 Togo
40 Benin
41 Cameroon
42 Equitorial Guinea
43 Gabon
44 Congo
1
120°
2
80°
3
40°
4
ARCTIC OCEAN
GREENLAND
Beaufort Sea
Baffin Bay
ALASKA
Yukon
Mackenzie
Back
ICELAND
Norwegia
Hudson Bay
Gulf of Alaska
CANADA
IRELAND
Newfoundland
Columbia
Missouri
Mississippi
Colorado
Arkansas
PORTUGAL
UNITED STATES OF AMERICA
NORTH
ATLANTIC
OCEAN
MOROCCO
CANARY ISLANDS
Rio Grande
WESTERN SAHARA
BAHAMAS
MEXICO
WEST INDIES
CUBA
DOMINICAN REPUBLIC
HAWAIIAN ISLANDS
JAMAICA
HAITI
BELIZE
PUERTO RICO
MAURITANIA
GUATEMALA
HONDURAS
SENEGAL
GAMBIA
EL SALVADOR
NICARAGUA
TRINIDAD & TOBAGO
GUINEA-BISSAU
COSTA RICA
VENEZUELA
PANAMA
Orinoco
GUINEA
SIERRA LEONE
LIBERIA
PACIFIC
COLOMBIA
GALAPAGOS ISLANDS
ECUADOR
Negro
Amazon
OCEAN
Madeira
Xingu
PERU
BRAZIL
São Francisco
SOUTH
POLYNESIA
BOLIVIA
Paraná
ATLANT
PARAGUAY
CHILE
OCEA
URUGUAY
ARGENTINA
FALKLAND/MALVINAS ISLANDS
South Georgia
G
H
10°
BAHAMA ISLANDS
GULF OF MEXICO
Andros I.
TURKS & CAICOS ISLANDS
Great Inagua
VIRGIN Is.
Barbuda
Antigua
Montserrat
Guadeloupe
Dominica
Martinique
St. Lucia
Barbados
St. Vincent
Grenada
Tobago
Trinidad
CUBA
DOMINICAN REPUBLIC
HAITI
PUERTO RICO
St. Kitts & Nevis
Yucatan Channel
Isla de la Juventud
GREATER ANTILLES
CAYMAN IS.
CAYMAN ISLANDS
Jamaica
JAMAICA
LESSER ANTILLES
CARIBBEAN SEA
BELIZE
Gulf of Honduras
HONDURAS
Netherlands Antilles
10
80°
11
70°
12
60°

5
40°
6
80°
7
120°
8
160°
9
A
B
C
D
E
80°
40°
0°
40°
ARCTIC OCEAN
SVALBARD
ZEMLYA FRANTSA IOSIFA
SEVERNAYA ZEMLYA
NOVOSIBIRSKIYE OSTROVO
Laptev Sea
East Siberian Sea
Chukchi Sea
Barents Sea
Novaya Zemlya
Kara Sea
Arctic Circle
Bering Strait
SWEDEN
FINLAND
RUSSIA
Dvina
Ob'
Yenisey
Nizhnyaya Tunguska
Lena
Indigirka
Kolyma
Aldan
Angara
Volga
Sea of Okhotsk
Bering Sea
ALEUTIAN ISLANDS
Don
Dnepr
Ural
Tobol
Ishim
Irtysh
KAZAKHSTAN
MONGOLIA
Caspian Sea
Aral Sea
Black Sea
GEORGIA
ARMENIA
AZERBAIJAN
UZBEKISTAN
KYRGYZSTAN
TURKMENISTAN
TAJIKISTAN
CHINA
Huang He
NORTH KOREA
Sea of Japan
SOUTH KOREA
JAPAN
TURKEY
SYRIA
IRAQ
IRAN
AFGHANISTAN
JORDAN
PAKISTAN
Indus
NEPAL
BHUTAN
Yellow Sea
East China Sea
LIBYA
EGYPT
Nile
Red Sea
SAUDI ARABIA
Ganges
Chang Jiang
PACIFIC OCEAN
Tropic of Cancer
TAIWAN
INDIA
BANGLADESH
MYANMAR
Irrawaddy
LAOS
OMAN
CHAD
ERITREA
YEMEN
SUDAN
Bay of Bengal
THAILAND
VIETNAM
South China Sea
CAMBODIA
PHILIPPINES
CENTRAL AFRICAN REPUBLIC
White Nile
ETHIOPIA
SOMALIA
SRI LANKA
BRUNEI
MALAYSIA
SINGAPORE
Celebes Sea
MICRONESIA
Uele
Congo
UGANDA
KENYA
MELANESIA
Kasai
BURUNDI
RWANDA
EAST INDIES
INDONESIA
PAPUA NEW GUINEA
ZAIRE
TANZANIA
INDIAN OCEAN
SOLOMON ISLANDS
ANGOLA
ZAMBIA
MALAWI
Coral Sea
VANUATU
FIJI
MADAGASCAR
NAMIBIA
ZIMBABWE
MOZAMBIQUE
MAURITIUS
RÉUNION
NEW CALEDONIA
Tropic of Capricorn
BOTSWANA
SWAZILAND
AUSTRALIA
Orange
LESOTHO
SOUTH AFRICA
North I.
Tasman Sea
NEW ZEALAND
South I.
Antarctic Circle
ANTARCTICA
11
12
13
14
15
16
17
18
19
20
21
22
23
24
25
26
27
28
29
30
31
32
33
34
35
44
0
5000 miles
0
5000 kilometres

56°
1
2
48°
40°
3
32°
4
24°
5
16°
6
8°
7
0°
8
8°
A
B
C
D
E
F
GREENLAND
GREENLAND SEA
Denmark Strait
Reykjavik
ICELAND
NORWEGIAN
SEA
FAROES IS.
SHETLAND IS.
NORWAY
Oslo
ATLANTIC
OCEAN
HEBRIDES
ORKNEY IS.
SCOTLAND
NORTH
SEA
Skagerrak
Edinburgh
DENMARK
Belfast
IRELAND
Dublin
Copenhagen
ENGLAND
WALES
Cardiff
London
NETHERLANDS
The Hague
Elbe
Berlin
Rhine
BELGIUM
Brussels
GERMANY
Paris
Luxembourg
Seine
LUXEMBOURG
Loire
Donau
FRANCE
Bay of
Biscay
Bern
SWITZERLAND
ALPS
MASSIF
CENTRAL
Rhône
Bilbao
SLOVENIA
Po
Duero
Andorra la Vella
Monaco
San Marino
PORTUGAL
Madrid
ANDORRA
Corsica
ITALY
Lisbon
Tajo
Barcelona
Rome
SPAIN
Sardinia
MADEIRA IS.
BALEARIC IS.
Strait of Gibraltar
Gibraltar
MEDITERRA
Sicily
Algiers
Rabat
Tunis
MOROCCO
Valletta
CANARY IS.
MALTA
Las Palmas
HAUT ATLAS
ATLAS SAHARIEN
TUNISIA
0
500
1000
miles

BARENTS SEA
Arctic Circle
WEST SIBERIAN PLAIN
URAL MOUNTAINS
Ob'
WHITE SEA
Dvina
Tobol
FINLAND
L.Onega
RUSSIA
L.Ladoga
Helsinki
KAZAKHSTAN
Tallinn
ESTONIA
Volga
LATVIA
Riga
Moscow
Vilnius
Sydar'ya
Minsk
Ural
BELARUS
Desna
Don
Pripyat
ARAL SEA
Warsaw
UZBEKISTAN
Kiev
Volga
UKRAINE
Dnestr
Dnepr
CARPATHIANS
MOLDOVA
Kishinev
Budapest
Prut
CASPIAN SEA
TURKMENISTAN
ROMANIA
CAUCASUS
Ashkhabad
Belgrade
Bucharest
GEORGIA
Tbilisi
Baku
BLACK SEA
AZERBAIJAN
Yerevan
BULGARIA
ARMENIA
Sofiya
Skopje
ELBURZ MOUNTAINS
Istanbul
Bosporus
MACEDONIA
Ankara
L.Van
Tehran
TURKEY
GREECE
Tigris
IRAN
Athens
SYRIA
Baghdad
Nicosia
Euphrates
CYPRUS
Beirut
LEBANON
Damascus
IRAQ
Crete
SEA
0 500 1000 kilometres
50°
42°
34°

24°
1
16°
2
8°
3
0°
4
8°
Aleureyri
Reykjavik
ICELAND
NORWEGIAN
SEA
Faroes Is.
Trondheim
Shetland Is.
NORWAY
Orkney Is.
Bergen
Hebrides
Oslo
John O'Groats
Inverness
SCOTLAND
Aberdeen
Dundee
NORTH
SEA
Skagerrak
Gothen
Londonderry
Edinburgh
Donegal
Alborg
Glasgow
Belfast
IRELAND
Newcastle-upon-Tyne
DENMARK
Galway
Carlisle
Isle of Man
Copenhagen
Limerick
Dublin
Holyhead
Killarney
Liverpool
IRISH
Cork
Sheffield
SEA
Kiel
Norwich
WALES
Birmingham
NETHERLANDS
Hamburg
Elbe
Cardiff
Bristol
ENGLAND
Utrecht
London
The Hague
Rotterdam
Berlin
Dover
Rhine
Penzance
GERMANY
BELGIUM
Brussels
0
500 miles

16° 6 24° 7 32° 8 40° 9 48° 10 56°

A
B
C

66°
58°
50°

Arctic Circle
Murmansk
Narvik
Lapland
WHITE SEA
Arkhangelsk
Oulu
N. Dvina
Kajaani
SWEDEN
Gulf of Bothnia
FINLAND
L.Onega
Tampere
L.Ladoga
Turku
Helsinki
St Petersburg
Stockholm
Tallinn
ESTONIA
BALTIC SEA
LATVIA
Riga
Moscow
LITHUANIA
Klaipéda
Smolensk
Vilnius
Mogilev
RUSSIA
Gdansk
Minsk
Desna
Don
BELARUS
POLAND
Pripyet
Brest
Warsaw

0 500 kilometres

1
8°
2
0°
3
Cardiff
Bristol
ENGLAND
London
Penzance
Dover
English Channel
Channel Is.
Brest
Utrech
The Hague
Rotterdam
Dortm
Rhine
Ostende
Antwerp
Calais
Ghent
Brussels
Maastricht
BELGIUM
Colo
Bon
Le Havre
Liege
Rouen
Fran
Seine
Paris
Luxembourg
LUXEMBOURG
Nantes
Loire
FRANCE
La Rochelle
Bay of Biscay
Bern
SWITZERL
Limoges
Geneva
Bordeaux
Lyons
Grenoble
Garonne
MASSIF CENTRAL
ALPS
Rhône
Bilbao
San Sebastian
Parn
PYRENEES
Toulouse
Ebro
Duero
PORTUGAL
Monaco
Marseilles
Andorra la Vella
Tyrrhen Sea
ANDORRA
Tagus
Lisbon
Tajo
Madrid
Toledo
Barcelona
Corsica
Guadiana
SPAIN
Valencia
Lagos
Cordoba
Faro
Seville
Ibiza
Balearic Is.
Sardinia
Alicante
SIERRA NEVADA
Marbella
Strait of Gibraltar
Gibraltar
Cagliar
MEDI
Algiers
Rabat
Annaba
Constantine
Tunis
MOROCCO
ATLAS SAHARIEN
TUNISIA

0 500 miles

4
16°
5
24°
6
32°
7
A
B
C
D
50°
42°
34°
POLAND
BELARUS
Pripyet
Hanover
Berlin
Poznań
Brest
Warsaw
ERMANY
Oder
Lublin
Kiev
Prague
Kraków
UKRAINE
Ostrava
Lvov
Dnepr
Nuremberg
CZECH REP.
Dnestr
Zilina
Donau
SLOVAKIA
CARPATHIANS
Munich
Linz
Vienna
Bratislava
MOLDOVA
Salzburg
Duna
Kishinev
Innsbruck
AUSTRIA
Prut
Odessa
Budapest
Graz
HUNGARY
SLOVENIA
Pécs
Arad
ROMANIA
Ljubljana
Zagreb
CROATIA
Tuzla
Resita
Bucharest
Belgrade
Marino
BOSNIA-HERZEGOVINA
BLACK SEA
Florence
Sarajevo
Danube
Varna
ITALY
YUGOSLAVIA
BULGARIA
Adriatic Sea
Pec
Sofiya
Pristina
Dubrovnik
Rome
Shkoder
Skopje
MACEDONIA
Istanbul
Tirana
Prilep
Naples
Taranto
Thessaloníki
ALBANIA
Bosporus
TURKEY
Aegean Sea
GREECE
Izmir
Pátrai
Palmero
Ionian Sea
Athens
Messina
Sicily
Antalya
Rhodes
Valletta
MALTA
MEDITERRANEAN SEA
Crete
0
500 kilometres

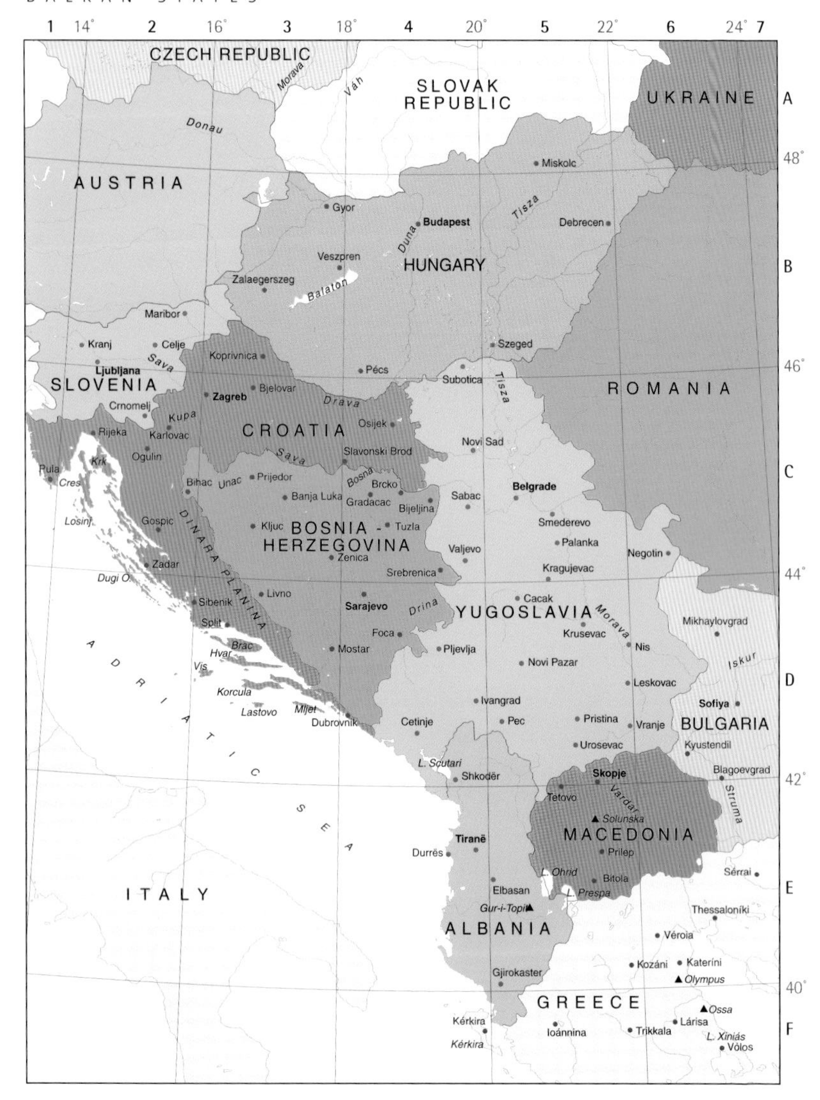
1
14°
2
16°
3
18°
4
20°
5
22°
6
24°
7
A
48°
B
46°
C
44°
D
42°
E
40°
F
CZECH REPUBLIC
Morava
Váh
SLOVAK REPUBLIC
UKRAINE
Donau
Miskolc
AUSTRIA
Gyor
Budapest
Tisza
Debrecen
Duna
Veszpren
HUNGARY
Zalaegerszeg
Balaton
Maribor
Kranj
Celje
Koprivnica
Szeged
Sava
Ljubljana
Pécs
Subotica
Tisza
SLOVENIA
Bjelovar
Zagreb
Drava
ROMANIA
Crnomelj
Kupa
Osijek
Rijeka
Karlovac
CROATIA
Novi Sad
Krk
Ogulin
Sava
Slavonski Brod
Pula
Cres
Bihac
Unac
Prijedor
Bosna
Brcko
Belgrade
Banja Luka
Gradacac
Sabac
Bijeljina
Losinj
Gospic
Kljuc
BOSNIA - HERZEGOVINA
Tuzla
Smederevo
DINARA PLANINA
Palanka
Valjevo
Zenica
Negotin
Zadar
Srebrenica
Kragujevac
Dugi O.
Livno
Cacak
Sibenik
Sarajevo
Drina
YUGOSLAVIA
Morava
Split
Mikhaylovgrad
Krusevac
Foca
Brac
Mostar
Pljevlja
Nis
Hvar
Vis
Novi Pazar
Iskur
ADRIATIC SEA
Leskovac
Korcula
Ivangrad
Sofiya
Lastovo
Mljet
Dubrovnik
Cetinje
Pec
Pristina
Vranje
BULGARIA
Urosevac
Kyustendil
L. Scutari
Shkodër
Skopje
Blagoevgrad
Tetovo
Vardar
Struma
Solunska
Tiranë
MACEDONIA
Durrës
Prilep
ITALY
L. Ohrid
Bitola
Sérrai
Elbasan
L. Prespa
Gur-i-Topit
Thessaloníki
ALBANIA
Véroia
Kozáni
Kateríni
Gjirokaster
Olympus
GREECE
Ossa
Kérkira
Ioánnina
Trikkala
Lárisa
L. Xiniás
Kérkira
Vólos

0
200 miles
0
200 kilometres

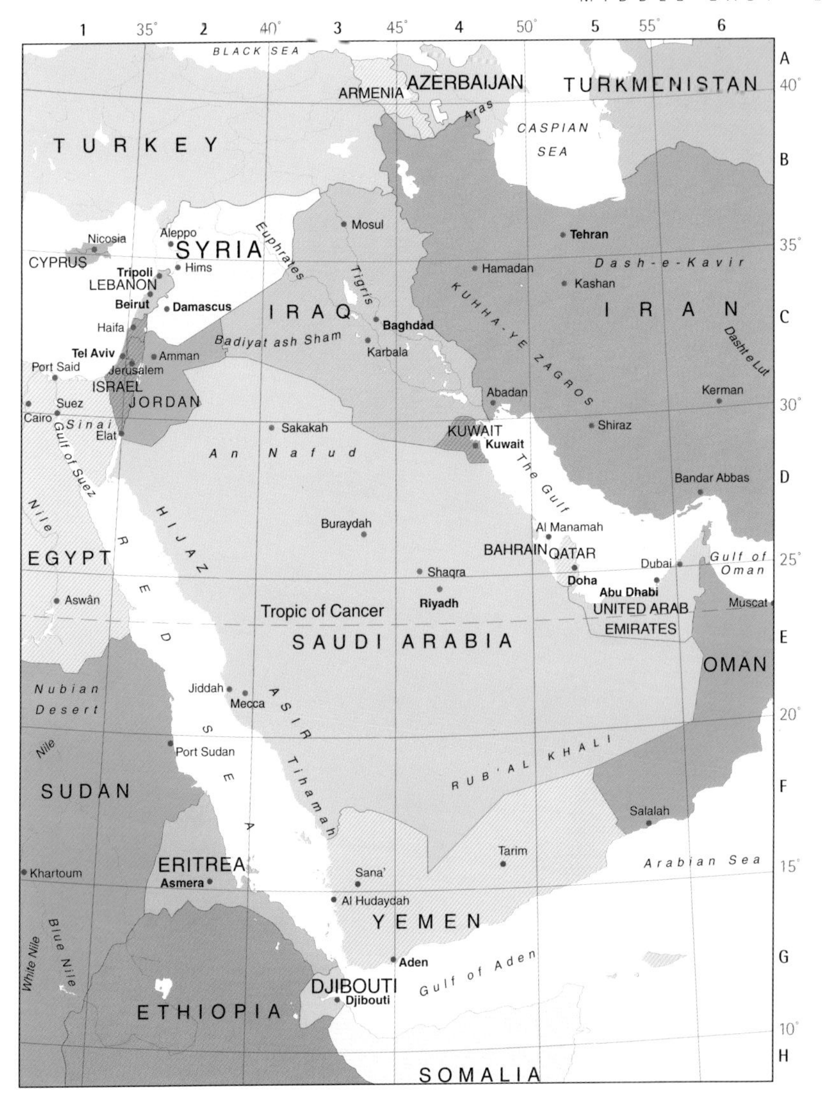

1
35°
2
40°
3
45°
4
50°
5
55°
6
A
40°
B
35°
C
30°
D
25°
E
20°
F
15°
G
10°
H
BLACK SEA
ARMENIA
AZERBAIJAN
TURKMENISTAN
Aras
CASPIAN SEA
TURKEY
Mosul
Tehran
Aleppo
Nicosia
SYRIA
Euphrates
CYPRUS
Tripoli
Hims
Tigris
Hamadan
Dash-e-Kavir
LEBANON
Kashan
Beirut
Damascus
IRAQ
IRAN
Haifa
Baghdad
KUHHA-YE ZAGROS
Tel Aviv
Badiyat ash Sham
Amman
Karbala
Dasht e Lut
Port Said
Jerusalem
ISRAEL
Abadan
Kerman
JORDAN
Suez
Cairo
Sinai
Sakakah
Shiraz
Elat
KUWAIT
Kuwait
An Nafud
The Gulf
Gulf of Suez
Bandar Abbas
Nile
HIJAZ
Buraydah
Al Manamah
EGYPT
R
BAHRAIN
QATAR
Dubai
Gulf of Oman
Shaqra
Doha
Abu Dhabi
Aswân
Riyadh
Tropic of Cancer
UNITED ARAB EMIRATES
Muscat
D
SAUDI ARABIA
OMAN
Nubian Desert
Jiddah
Mecca
ASIR
S
Nile
Port Sudan
RUB' AL KHALI
E
SUDAN
Tihamah
Salalah
A
Tarim
ERITREA
Arabian Sea
Khartoum
Asmera
Sana'
Al Hudaydah
YEMEN
Blue Nile
White Nile
Aden
Gulf of Aden
DJIBOUTI
Djibouti
ETHIOPIA
SOMALIA
0
500 miles
0
500 kilometres

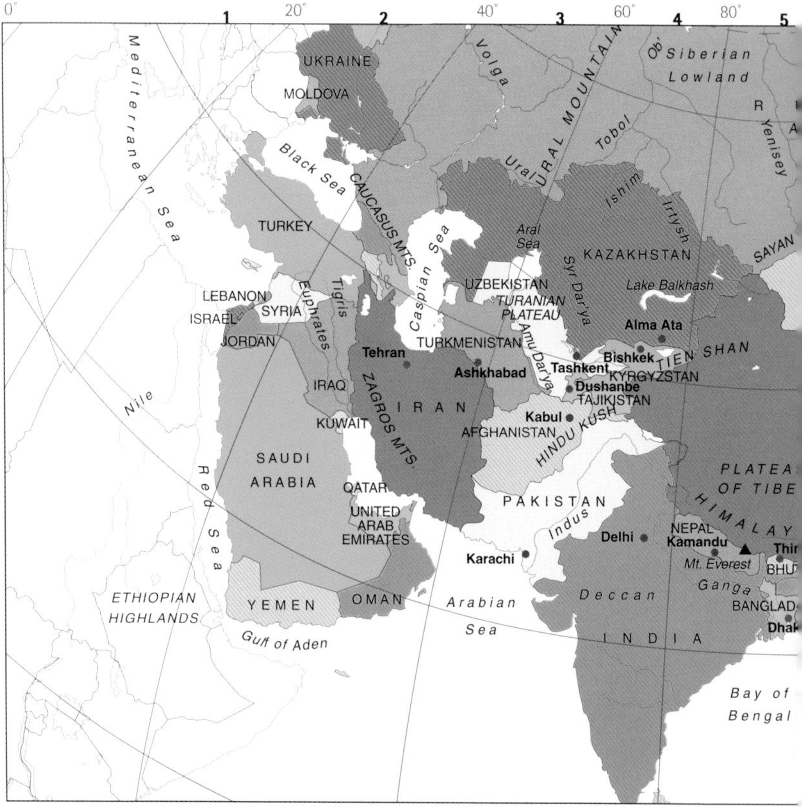

0° 1 20° 2 40° 3 60° 4 80° 5

UKRAINE
MOLDOVA
Volga
URAL MOUNTAINS
Ob'
Siberian Lowland
R
A
Yenisey
Tobol
Ural
Mediterranean Sea
Black Sea
CAUCASUS MTS.
Ishim
Irtysh
TURKEY
Caspian Sea
Aral Sea
KAZAKHSTAN
SAYAN
Syr Dar'ya
Lake Balkhash
UZBEKISTAN
TURANIAN PLATEAU
LEBANON
SYRIA
Euphrates
Tigris
ISRAEL
JORDAN
Amu Dar'ya
Alma Ata
TURKMENISTAN
Tehran
Ashkhabad
Tashkent
Bishkek
TIEN SHAN
KYRGYZSTAN
IRAQ
ZAGROS MTS.
IRAN
Dushanbe
TAJIKISTAN
Nile
KUWAIT
Kabul
HINDU KUSH
AFGHANISTAN
SAUDI ARABIA
Red Sea
PLATEAU OF TIBET
QATAR
PAKISTAN
HIMALAYA
UNITED ARAB EMIRATES
Indus
NEPAL
Delhi
Kamandu
Karachi
Mt. Everest
Thi
BHU
ETHIOPIAN HIGHLANDS
YEMEN
OMAN
Arabian Sea
Deccan
Ganga
BANGLAD
Dhak
Gulf of Aden
INDIA
Bay of Bengal

0 1000 miles

0 1000 kilometres

1 2 3

100° 110° 120°
George Town
Kuala Terengganu
Sanda
Ipoh
Bandar Seri Begawan
BRUNEI
Medan
Kelang
Kuala Lumpur
Nantuna Besar
Strait of Malacca
MALAYSIA
Johor
SINGAPORE
Kapuas
Borneo
Makassar St
Sumatra
Pontianak
Padang
Hari
Balikpapan
Jambi
Bangka
Barito
PEG. BARISAN
Palembang
Belitung
IND
Banjarmasin
JAVA SEA
Ujung Pandang
Jakarta
Bandung
Java
Surabaya
FLOR
Bali
Lombok
Malang
Sumbawa
Mataram

0 500 miles

0 500 kilometres

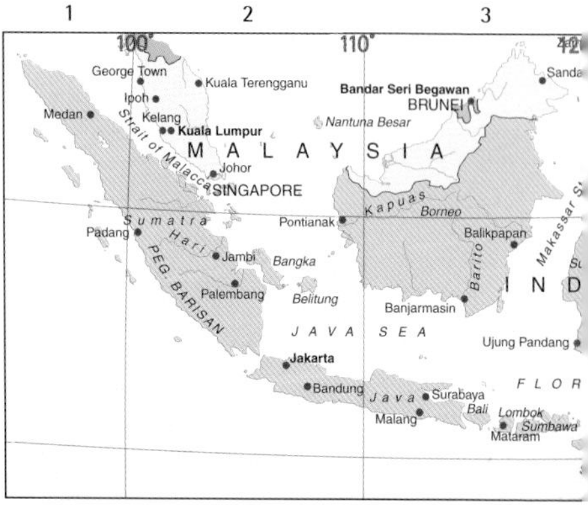

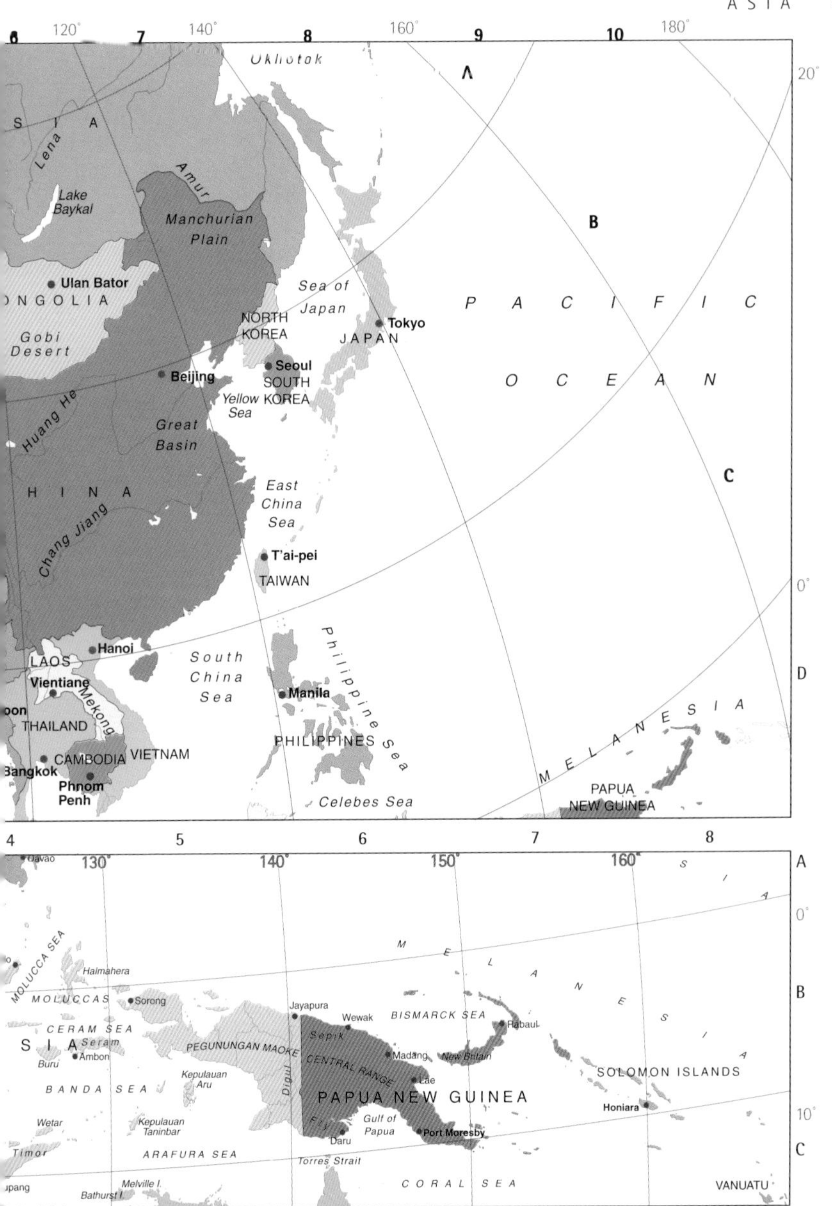

Okhotok
Lena
Lake Baykal
Amur
Manchurian Plain
Ulan Bator
ONGOLIA
Gobi Desert
Sea of Japan
NORTH KOREA
Tokyo
JAPAN
P A C I F I C
O C E A N
Seoul
SOUTH KOREA
Beijing
Yellow Sea
Huang He
Great Basin
CHINA
East China Sea
Chang Jiang
T'ai-pei
TAIWAN
Hanoi
LAOS
Vientiane
South China Sea
Manila
Philippine Sea
THAILAND
Mekong
PHILIPPINES
CAMBODIA
VIETNAM
Bangkok
Phnom Penh
Celebes Sea
MELANESIA
PAPUA NEW GUINEA
Davao
MOLUCCA SEA
Halmahera
MOLUCCAS
Sorong
CERAM SEA
Seram
Ambon
Buru
BANDA SEA
Jayapura
Wewak
BISMARCK SEA
Rabaul
Sepik
PEGUNUNGAN MAOKE
CENTRAL RANGE
Madang
New Britain
Kepulauan Aru
Digul
Lae
PAPUA NEW GUINEA
SOLOMON ISLANDS
Honiara
Wetar
Kepulauan Tanimbar
Fly
Gulf of Papua
Daru
Port Moresby
Timor
ARAFURA SEA
Torres Strait
CORAL SEA
Melville I.
Bathurst I.
VANUATU

1 60° 2 65° 3 70° 4 75° 5 80° 6 85° 7
TARIM PENDI
Sheberghan
Herat
HINDU KUSH
ALTUN S
AFGHANISTAN
Hotan
Farah
Kabul
Khyber Pass
KARAKORAM
KUNLAN
Srinagar
Islamabad
Qandahar
SULAJMAN RANG
Indus
QING ZAN
Zahedan
Quetta
Lahore
Multan
GANGDISE SHAN
PAKISTAN
Sutlej
HIMALAYA
Bahawalpur
KIRTHAR RA.
Sukkur
Indus
PLATEAU OF TI
Gwadar
Xigaze
New Delhi
Annapurna
Hyderabad
Mt Everest
NEPAL
Karachi
Jodhpur
Jaipur
Yamuna
Katmandu
Ajmer
Lucknow
Ghagara
BH
Kanpur
Allahabad
Varanasi
Udaipur
Ganges
Gulf of Kachc
Patna
Ahmadabad
Son
BANG
Jamnagar
Bhavnagar
Vadodara
Narmada
Surat
Jamshedpur
Gulf of Khambhat
INDIA
Calcutta
ARABIAN
SEA
Nagpur
Raipur
Mahanadi
Mouths of t
Bombay
DECCAN
Cuttack
Pune
Godavari
WESTERN GHATS
EASTERN GHAT
Solapur
Kolhapur
Hyderabad
Vishakhapatnam
Krishna
Vijayawada
BAY OF
BENGA
Hubli-Dharwar
Goa
Kurnool
Nellore
Mangalore
Bangalore
Madras
Mysore
LACCADIVE IS.
0
500 miles
Kozhikode
Coimbatore
Tiruchchirappalli
0
500 kilometres
Madurai
Jaffna
Thiruvananthapuram
Trincomalee
C. Comorin
Gulf of Mann
SRI LANKA
INDIAN OCEAN
Colombo
Kandy

95° 9 100° 10 105° 11 110° 12 115° 13 120° 14
A
B
C
D
E
F
30°
25°
20°
15°
10°
0°
YELLOW SEA
QILIAN SHAN
Qinghai Hu
Hwang Ho
Zhengzhou
Luoyang
Lanzhou
Shanghai
Xi'an
Huang He
HUA SHAN
Hangzhou
XILSHA
BAYAN HAR SHAN
Tongtian He
DABA SHAN
CHINA
Chang Jiang
Wuhan
Poyang Hu
NGGULA SHAN
Nanchang
Dongting Hu
Chengdu
Qamdo
RED BASIN
Chongqing
Changsha
Fuzhou
HENGDUAN SHAN
DALOU SHAN
Hengyang
Guiyang
Tropic of Cancer
Shantou
aputra
NAGA HILLS
auhati
Xiaguan
Kunming
Liuzhou
Guangzhou
Hong Kong
Macau
Nanning
Dongsha Qundao
Imphal
Zhanjiang
BURMA
Hanoi
Haiphong
Haikou
ARAKAN YOMA
Irrawaddy
Mandalay
PEGU YOMA
Gulf of Tongkin
Hainan
Louang Prabang
TANEN R.
Vinh
LAOS
Chiang Mai
Prome
M.Lampang
Vientiane
Mekong
DAWNA RANGE
Hue
Da Nang
Henzada
THAILAND
Bassein
Rangoon
Moulmein
VIETNAM
Nakhon Ratchasima
Qui Nhon
Mouths of the Irrawaddy
Gulf of Martaban
PHANOM DANG RAEK
Chu Yang Sin
BILAUKTAUNG R.
CAMBODIA
Tavoy
Bangkok
Nha Trang
Battambang
Kampong Cham
Phnom Penh
Mergui
Ho Chi Minh City
Can Tho
SOUTH CHINA SEA
Andaman Sea
MERGUI ARCHIP.
Gulf of Thailand
Mouths of the Mekong
egree Channel
Mui Bai Bung
Nakhon Si Thammarat
NICOBAR IS.
Phuket
Songkhla
Gt. Nicobar

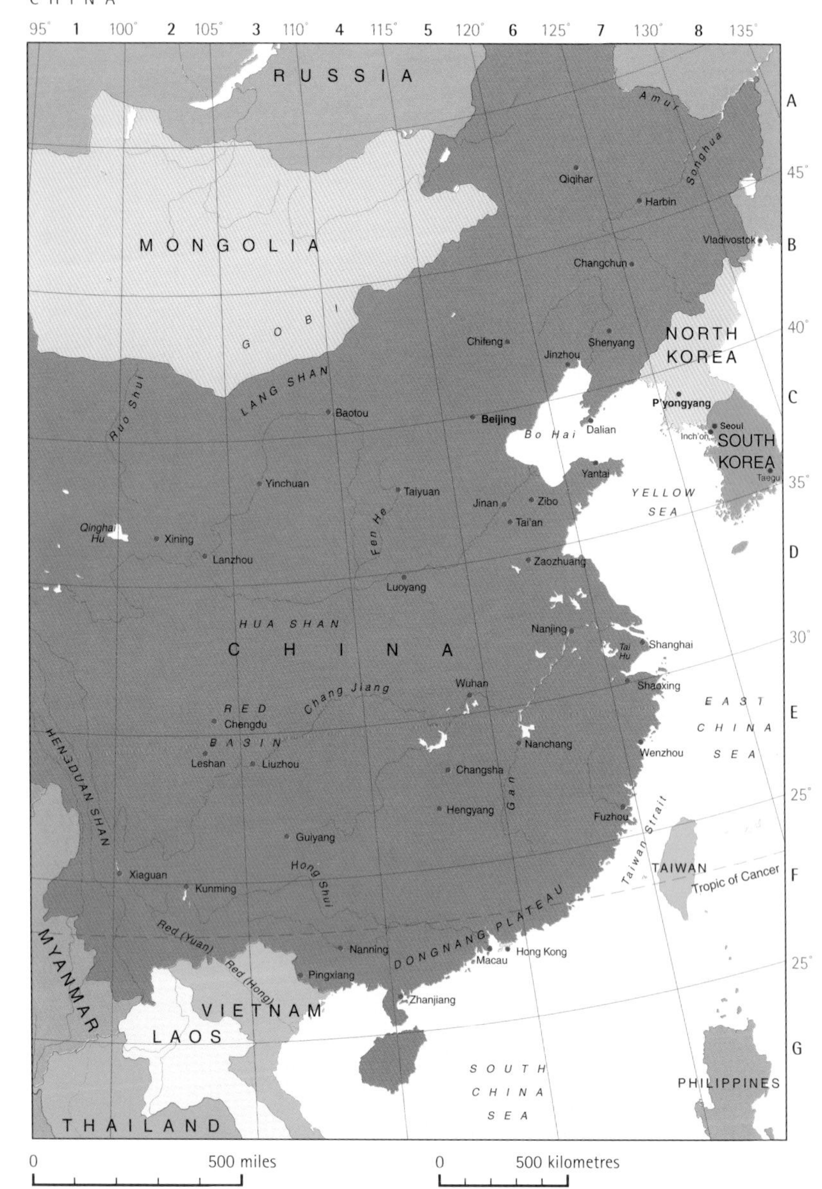
95°
1
100°
2
105°
3
110°
4
115°
5
120°
6
125°
7
130°
8
135°
A
B
C
D
E
F
G
45°
40°
35°
30°
25°
RUSSIA
Amur
Songhua
Qiqihar
Harbin
Vladivostok
MONGOLIA
Changchun
GOBI
Chifeng
Shenyang
NORTH KOREA
Jinzhou
LANG SHAN
Ruo Shui
Baotou
Beijing
Dalian
P'yongyang
Seoul
Inch'on
SOUTH KOREA
Bo Hai
Yantai
Taegu
Yinchuan
Taiyuan
YELLOW SEA
Jinan
Zibo
Tai'an
Qinghai Hu
Xining
Fen He
Lanzhou
Zaozhuang
Luoyang
HUA SHAN
Nanjing
CHINA
Shanghai
Tai Hu
Wuhan
Shaoxing
Chang Jiang
RED BASIN
Chengdu
EAST CHINA SEA
HENGDUAN SHAN
Nanchang
Leshan
Liuzhou
Wenzhou
Changsha
Gan
Hengyang
Fuzhou
Taiwan Strait
Guiyang
TAIWAN
Hong Shui
Xiaguan
Kunming
Tropic of Cancer
Red (Yuan)
DONGNANG PLATEAU
MYANMAR
Nanning
Macau
Hong Kong
Red (Hong)
Pingxiang
Zhanjiang
VIETNAM
LAOS
SOUTH CHINA SEA
PHILIPPINES
THAILAND
0
500 miles
0
500 kilometres

128°
2
132°
3
136°
4
140°
5
144°
6
A
B
C
D
E
44°
40°
36°
32°
RUSSIA
HINA
ORTH
OREA
UTH
REA
La P rouse Strait
Wakkanai
Hokkaido
Sapporo
Kushiro
Uchiura-Wan
Hakodate
Tsugaru-Kaikyo
Aomori
Hachinohe
SEA OF
JAPAN
Akita
Miyako
Sakata
Yamagata
Sendai
Sado-Shima
Niigata
Abukuma
Ullung Do
HONSHU
JAPAN
Iwaki
Hitachi
Toyama
Takasaki
Fukui
Haku-San
Yariga-Take
Oki-Shoto
Tokyo
Choshi
Matsue
Ibi
Shirani-San
Gifu
Fuji
Fuji-San
Yokohama
Toyota
Kyoto
rea Strait
Okayama
Kobe
Hiroshima
Sakai
Hamamatsu
O-Shima
Miyake-Jima
Shimonoseki
Tokushima
Kii-Suido
Fukuoka
Matsuyama
Shikoku
Kochi
Sasebo
Omuta
Bungo-Suido
Hachijo-Jima
Nagasaki
Kyushu
Sendai
Miyazaki
Kagoshima
PACIFIC
OCEAN
Tanega
Yaku
0
500 miles
0
500 kilometres

1
20°
2
10°
3
0°
A
30°
B
20°
C
10°
D
0°
E
10°
F
20°
G
30°
H
MOROCCO
ATLAS MOUNTAINS
ALGER
WESTERN SAHARA
Tropic of Cancer
Mt.
MAURITANIA
SAHARA
Nouakchott
MALI
Sénégal
Niger
SENEGAL
Dakar
GAMBIA
Banjul
Bissau
GUINEA BISSAU
Bamako
BURKINO FASO
Niamey
Ouagadougou
GUINEA
BENIN
Conakry
GHANA
Freetown
SIERRA LEONE
IVORY COAST
TOGO
Lomé
Lagos
Monrovia
LIBERIA
Abidjan
Accra
Porto Novo
GULF OF GUINEA
EQUATORIA
ATLANTIC OCEAN
Tropic of Capricorn
0
500
1000 miles
0
500
1000 kilometres

10° 5 20° 6 30° 7 40° 8 50° 9 60

NISIA
Tripoli
MEDITERRANEAN SEA
ISRAEL
JORDAN
Cairo
Suez
LIBYA
Libyan Desert
Western Desert
Nile
EGYPT
SAUDI ARABIA
RED SEA
ERT
TIBESTI
Nubian Desert
GER
CHAD
Khartoum
Asmera
ERITREA
Ndjamena
DJIBOUTI
Djibouti
Socotra
Caseyr
Berbera
SUDAN
A
Blue Nile
Addis Ababa
SOMALIA
ETHIOPIAN HIGHLANDS
ETHIOPIA
CENTRAL AFRICAN REPUBLIC
White Nile
aoundé
Bangui
Bomu
EROON
Congo
UGANDA
KENYA
Kampala
Mogadishu
reville
Tana
BON
CONGO
ZAIRE
RWANDA
Kigali
Lake Victoria
Nairobi
Mwanza
Bujumburo
INDIAN OCEAN
razzaville
Kinshasa
BURUNDI
Kilimanjaro
SEYCHELLES
Zanzibar
Dodoma
anda
ANGOLA PLATEAU
TANZANIA
Farquhar Is.
ANGOLA
COMOROS
MALAWI
Lilongwe
ZAMBIA
Cubango
Lusaka
Blantyre
Zambesi
MOZAMBIQUE
Mozambique Channel
Harare
NAMIBIA
ZIMBABWE
Antananarivo
MADAGASCAR
Mauritius
Namib Desert
Windhoek
BOTSWANA
Limpopo
Réunion
Gaborone
Maputo
Johannesburg
Mbabane
SWAZILAND
Maseru
LESOTHO
DRAKENSBERG
Durban
SOUTH AFRICA
Cape Town
Cape of Good Hope
Cape St. Francis

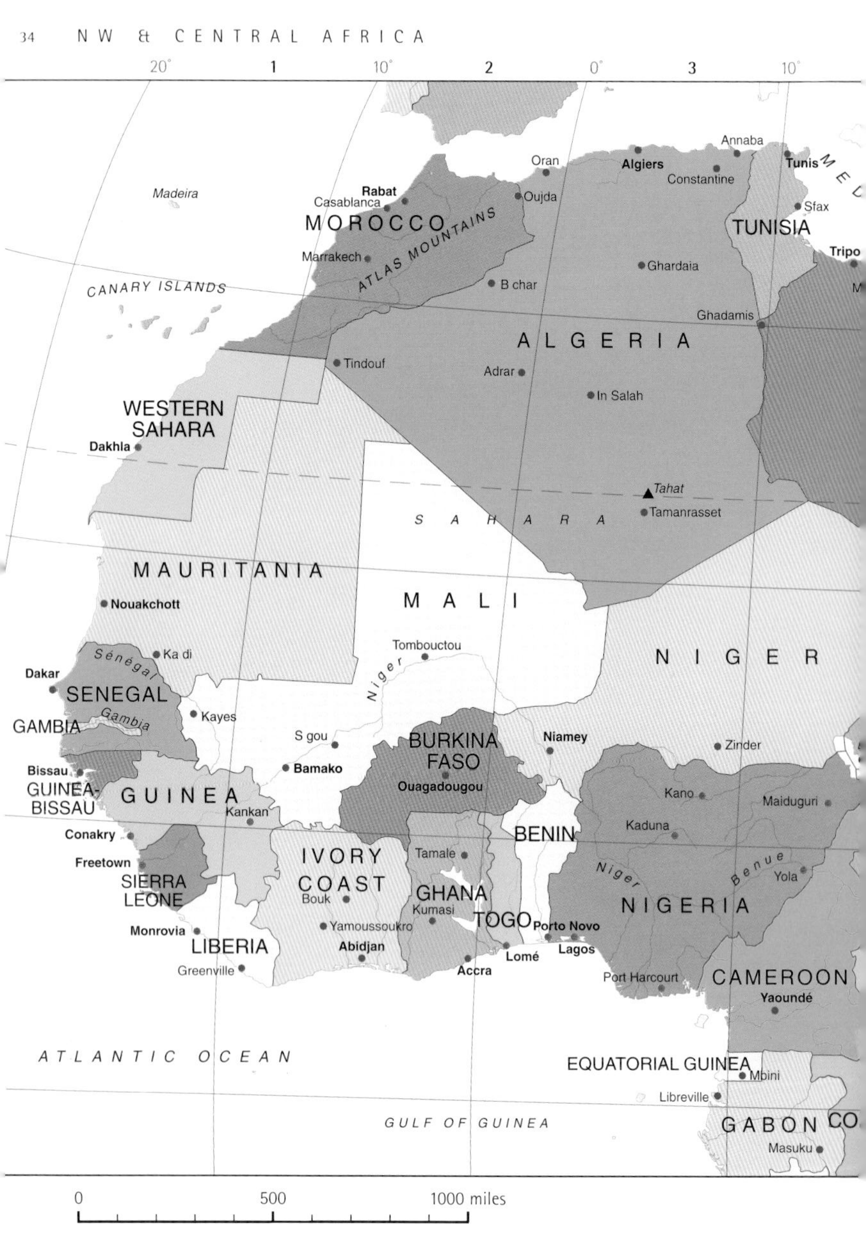
20°
1
10°
2
0°
3
10°
Madeira
CANARY ISLANDS
Rabat
Casablanca
MOROCCO
ATLAS MOUNTAINS
Marrakech
Oran
Oujda
Algiers
Annaba
Constantine
Tunis
Sfax
TUNISIA
Tripo
Ghardaia
B char
Ghadamis
ALGERIA
Tindouf
Adrar
In Salah
WESTERN SAHARA
Dakhla
Tahat
Tamanrasset
SAHARA
MAURITANIA
Nouakchott
MALI
Tombouctou
Niger
NIGER
Sénégal
Ka di
Dakar
SENEGAL
Gambia
GAMBIA
Kayes
S gou
Bamako
BURKINA FASO
Ouagadougou
Niamey
Zinder
Kano
Maiduguri
Bissau
GUINEA-BISSAU
GUINEA
Kankan
Conakry
Freetown
SIERRA LEONE
IVORY COAST
Bouk
Yamoussoukro
Abidjan
Tamale
GHANA
Kumasi
Accra
TOGO
Lomé
BENIN
Porto Novo
Lagos
Kaduna
Niger
Benue
Yola
NIGERIA
Port Harcourt
CAMEROON
Yaoundé
Monrovia
LIBERIA
Greenville
ATLANTIC OCEAN
EQUATORIAL GUINEA
Mbini
Libreville
GULF OF GUINEA
GABON
CO
Masuku
0
500
1000 miles

20°
5
30°
6
40°
7
50
RANEAN SEA
LEBANON
ISRAEL
JORDAN
Derna
f of Sirte
Port Said
Cairo
Suez
EGYPT
Great Sand Sea
LIBYAN DESERT
BYA
Nile
Asy t
Qena
RED SEA
ropic of Cancer
Asw n
Lake Nasser
SAUDI ARABIA
Jiddah
Nubian Desert
Port Sudan
Faya-Largeau
Nile
SUDAN
CHAD
Kassala
ERITREA
Asmera
YEMEN
Khartoum
Ab ch
Geneina
El Obeid
Kosti
Blue Nile
ETHIOPIAN PLATEAU
Gonder
Lake Tana
DJIBOUTI
Djibouti
Gulf of Aden
Berbera
SOMALIA
Addis Ababa
White Nile
Gore
ENTRAL AFRICAN REPUBLIC
ETHIOPIA
Webi
Bangassou
Uele
Nimule
Isha Baidoa
Lisala
Congo
UGANDA
Jubba
Mogadishu
ZAIRE
Lake Albert
Kampala
KENYA
Mbandaka
Lake Edward
Lake Victoria
Kisumu
Nairobi
INDIAN OCEAN
Kismayu
A
B
C
D
E
30°
20°
10°
0°
0
500
1000 kilometres

10°
1
20°
2
Mayumba
Brazzaville
Pointe-Noire
Kinshasa
Zaire
Cabinda
Matadi
Ponta do Padrão
Lukenie
Kasai
Kwilu
Kwango
Kikwit
ZAIRE
Lomami
Tshikapa
Kananga
Kasai
Lubilash
Kamina
Luanda
Ponta des Palmeirinhas
Caúgula
Saurimo
Cuanza
Gunza
Gabela
Sumbe
Cassai
Likasi
Lobito
Camacupa
Luena
Benguela
ANGOLA
Kitwe
Lubango
ZAMBIA
Namibe
Tombua
Cunene
Cubango
Cuito
Cuando
Zambezi
Kafue
Livingstone
Cape Fria
Okavango Basin
Grootfontein
Maun
NAMIB DESERT
Lake Ngami
Francistown
Omaruru
Kariblb
BOTSWANA
Serowe
Tropic of Capricorn
Walvis Bay
Windhoek
KALAHARI
NAMIBIA
DESERT
Gaborone
Lüderitz
Keetmanshoop
Karasburg
Vaal
Upington
Alexander Bay
Kimberley
Port Nolloth
Orange
Bloemfontein
SOUTH AFRICA
ATLANTIC OCEAN
Victoria West
Queenstown
Cape Town
Oudtshoorn
Port Elizabeth
Cape of Good Hope
Hermanus
Cape Agulhas

30°
3
40°
4
50°
5
Mwanza
NDI
Bujumbura
Shinyanga
Kilimanjaro
Mombasa
Kigoma
Same
Tabora
Pemba I.
ake
anyika
TANZANIA
Zanzibar
Zanzibar I.
INDIAN OCEAN
A
Dodoma
Dar es Salaam
Lake
Rukwa
Mafia I.
Mbala
Kilwa Masoko
10°
Cabo Delgado
Ruvuma
Lake
gweulu
Cap d'Ambre
Comoros Islands
Lake
Nyasa
Antseranana
Chipata
Lilongwe
Lúrio
MALAWI
B
Zambezi
Nampula
Moçambique
Mahajanga
Tete
Blantyre
Mozambique Channel
Maroantsetra
Harare
MOZAMBIQUE
MADAGASCAR
BWE
Antananarivo
Beira
asvingo
Morondava
20°
Save
Fianarantsoa
Limpopo
Ponta São Sebastião
Toliara
Inhambane
Betioky
Maputo
C
Mbabane
SWAZILAND
Cap Sainte-Marie
Durban
30°
0
500
1000 miles
D
0
500
1000 kilometres

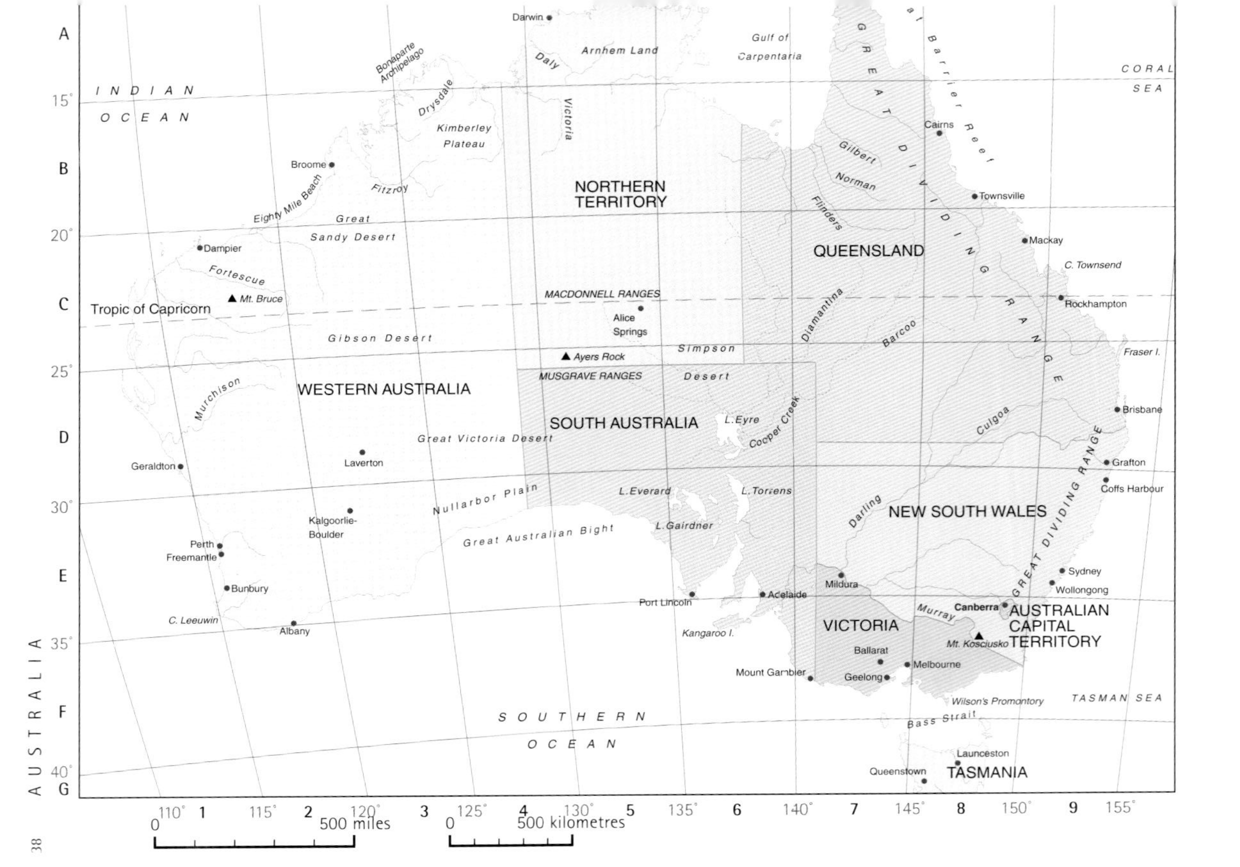
A
B
C
D
E
F
G
15°
20°
25°
30°
35°
40°
110°
115°
120°
125°
130°
135°
140°
145°
150°
155°
1
2
3
4
5
6
7
8
9
0
500 miles
0
500 kilometres
Darwin
Arnhem Land
Daly
Gulf of Carpentaria
Bonaparte Archipelago
CORAL SEA
INDIAN OCEAN
Drysdale
Victoria
Kimberley Plateau
GREAT DIVIDING RANGE
Great Barrier Reef
Cairns
Gilbert
Broome
Norman
Fitzroy
NORTHERN TERRITORY
Townsville
Eighty Mile Beach
Flinders
Great Sandy Desert
Dampier
QUEENSLAND
Mackay
Fortescue
C. Townsend
Mt. Bruce
MACDONNELL RANGES
Diamantina
Tropic of Capricorn
Alice Springs
Rockhampton
Gibson Desert
Simpson Desert
Barcoo
Ayers Rock
Fraser I.
MUSGRAVE RANGES
Murchison
WESTERN AUSTRALIA
SOUTH AUSTRALIA
L.Eyre
Cooper Creek
Brisbane
Culgoa
Great Victoria Desert
Geraldton
Laverton
Grafton
Coffs Harbour
L.Everard
L.Torrens
Nullarbor Plain
NEW SOUTH WALES
Darling
Kalgoorlie-Boulder
L.Gairdner
Great Australian Bight
Perth
Freemantle
Sydney
Wollongong
Mildura
Bunbury
Adelaide
Port Lincoln
Canberra
AUSTRALIAN CAPITAL TERRITORY
Murray
C. Leeuwin
Albany
VICTORIA
Kangaroo I.
Mt. Kosciusko
Ballarat
Melbourne
Mount Gambier
Geelong
Wilson's Promontory
TASMAN SEA
SOUTHERN OCEAN
Bass Strait
Launceston
Queenstown
TASMANIA

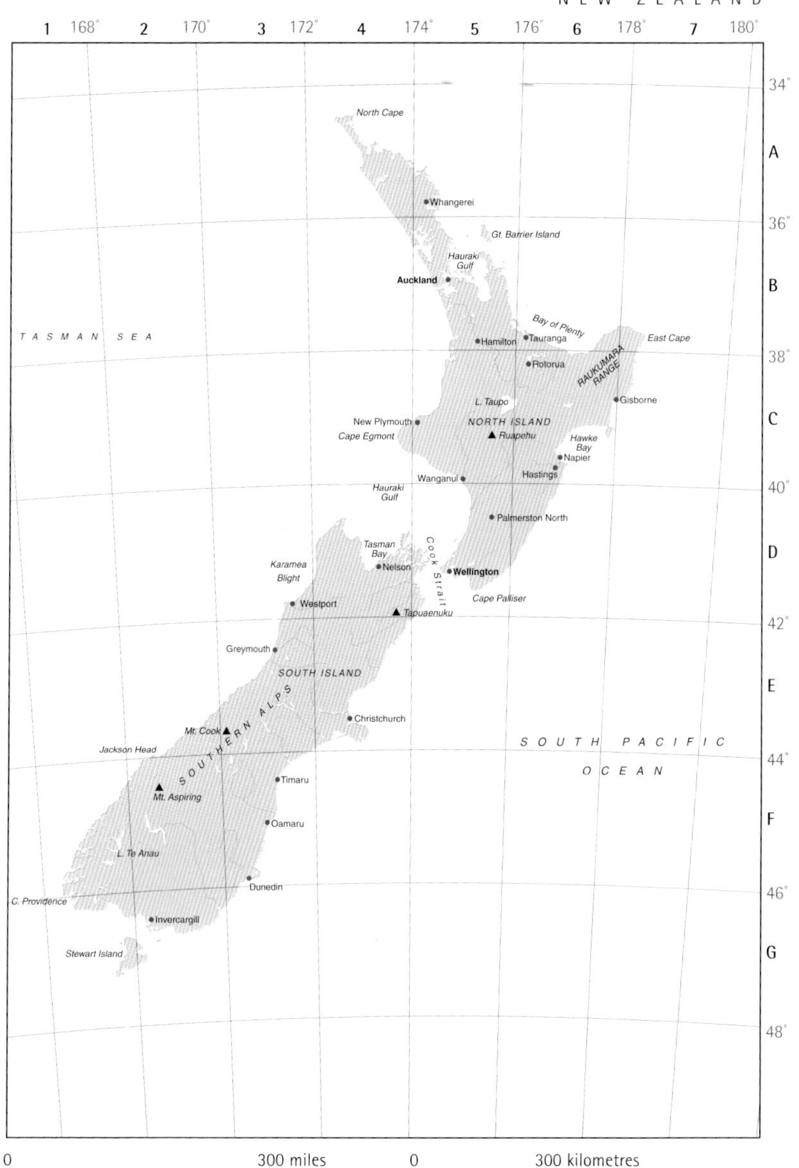
1 168°
2 170°
3 172°
4 174°
5 176°
6 178°
7 180°
34°
36°
38°
40°
42°
44°
46°
48°
A
B
C
D
E
F
G
North Cape
Whangerei
Gt. Barrier Island
Hauraki Gulf
Auckland
Bay of Plenty
TASMAN SEA
Hamilton
Tauranga
East Cape
Rotorua
RAUKUMARA RANGE
L. Taupo
Gisborne
New Plymouth
NORTH ISLAND
Cape Egmont
Ruapehu
Hawke Bay
Napier
Hastings
Wanganui
Hauraki Gulf
Palmerston North
Tasman Bay
Cook Strait
Karamea Blight
Nelson
Wellington
Cape Palliser
Westport
Tapuaenuku
Greymouth
SOUTH ISLAND
SOUTHERN ALPS
Christchurch
Mt. Cook
Jackson Head
SOUTH PACIFIC OCEAN
Timaru
Mt. Aspiring
Oamaru
L. Te Anau
Dunedin
C. Providence
Invercargill
Stewart Island
0
300 miles
0
300 kilometres

180° 1 160° 2 140° 3 120° 4

ARCTIC OCEAN

CHUKCHI SEA

BERING SEA

BEAUFORT SEA

St. Lawrence Island

Yukon

Porcupine

ALASKA (USA)

Mt. McKinley

Anchorage

MCKENZIE MOUNTAINS

Great Bear Lake

ALEUTIAN ISLANDS

YUKON TERRITORY

NORT

GULF OF ALASKA

Great Slave Lake

BRITISH COLUMBIA

ROCKY MOUNTAINS

ALBERTA

CA

SASKATCHEWA

Seattle

Mt. Rainier

WASHINGTON

Missouri

Salem

CASCADE RANGE

Helena

MONTANA

OREGON

Boise

IDAHO

WYOMING

SIERRA NEVADA

Platte

Great Salt Lake

Cheyenne

Carson City

Salt Lake City

San Francisco

NEVADA

UTAH

Denver

Colorado

COLORADO

Ark

Mt. Whitney

Las Vegas

CALIFORNIA

UNITED STAT

Los Angeles

ARIZONA

Santa Fe

NEW MEXICO

Tropic of Cancer

Phoenix

El Paso

Baja California

GULF OF CALIFORNIA

0 500 1000 miles

0 500 1000 kilometres

5 80° 6 60° 7 40° 8 20°
GREENLAND
A
B
C
D
10°
20°
30°
Baffin Bay
Baffin Island
TORIES
LABRADOR SEA
Cape Chidley
Hudson Bay
QUEBEC
TOBA
NEWFOUNDLAND
D A
St. John's
Cape Race
ONTARIO
PRINCE EDWARD IS.
NEW BRUNSWICK
NOVA SCOTIA
Halifax
MAINE
Augusta
Cape Sable
L. Superior
L. Huron
MINNESOTA
VERMONT
Montpelier
NEW HAMPSHIRE
Concord
St. Paul
MICHIGAN
Boston
MASSACHUSETTS
Cape Cod
WISCONSIN
L. Michigan
Mississippi
NEW YORK
Hartford
Providence
RHODE ISLAND
CONNECTICUT
Madison
Lansing
Detroit
New York
PENNSYLVANIA
Trenton
IOWA
Harrisburg
NEW JERSEY
Des Moines
Chicago
OHIO
Columbus
Annapolis
Dover
DELAWARE
WASHINGTON D.C.
MARYLAND
INDIANA
Springfield
WEST VIRGINIA
Indianapolis
Charleston
Richmond
ILLINOIS
Frankfort
VIRGINIA
St. Louis
KENTUCKY
Cape Hatteras
BERMUDA
MISSOURI
NORTH CAROLINA
Raleigh
AMERICA
Nashville
TENNESSEE
ATLANTIC OCEAN
AHOMA
ARKANSAS
Columbia
Cape Fear
oma City
Little Rock
Red
Alabama
SOUTH CAROLINA
Atlanta
GEORGIA
Jackson
Dallas
LOUISIANA
Montgomery
ALABAMA
MISSISSIPPI
Jacksonville
Houston
New Orleans
Orlando
Mississippi Delta
FLORIDA
Tropic of Cancer
Miami
BAHAMAS

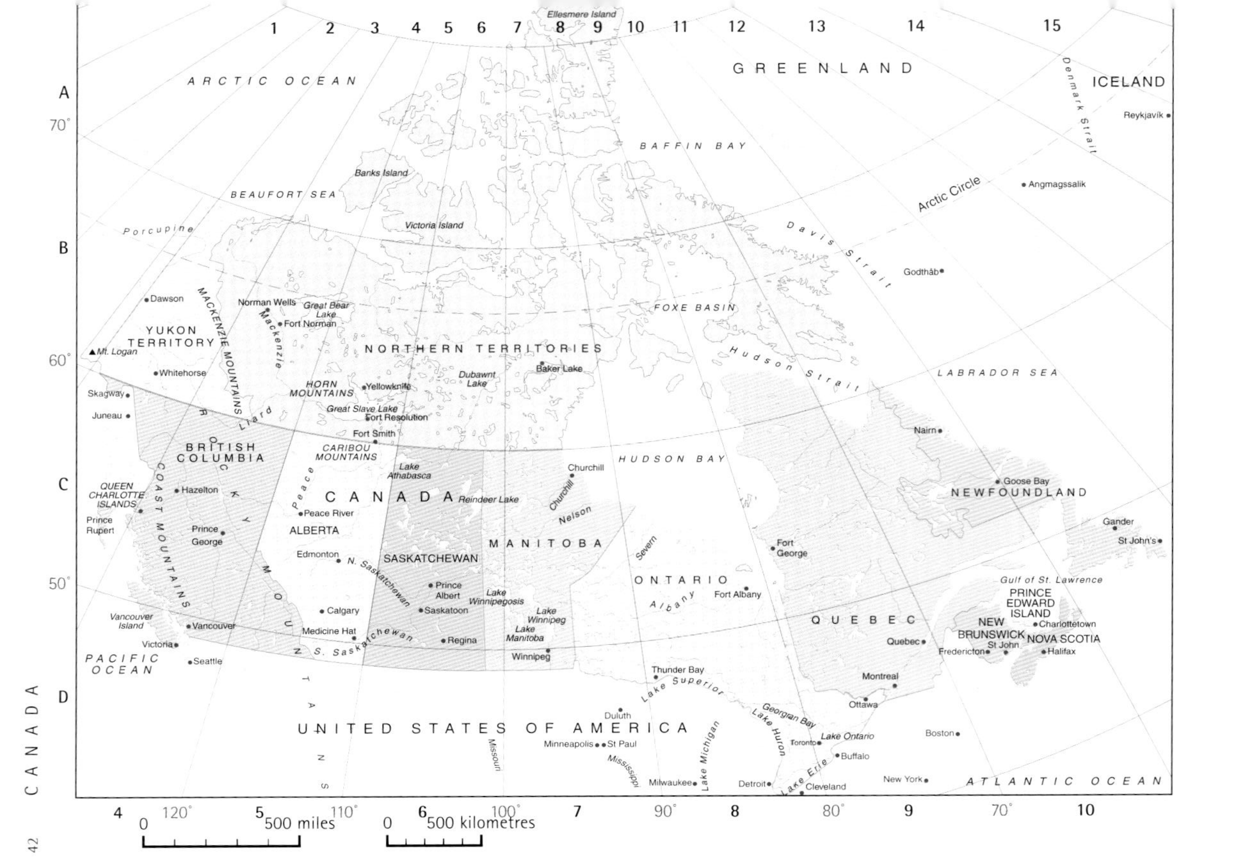

Ellesmere Island
ARCTIC OCEAN
GREENLAND
ICELAND
Reykjavík
Denmark Strait
BAFFIN BAY
Banks Island
BEAUFORT SEA
Arctic Circle
Angmagssalik
Porcupine
Victoria Island
Davis Strait
Godthåb
Dawson
MACKENZIE MOUNTAINS
Norman Wells
Great Bear Lake
Mackenzie
Fort Norman
YUKON TERRITORY
Mt. Logan
NORTHERN TERRITORIES
FOXE BASIN
Hudson Strait
Whitehorse
Baker Lake
Dubawnt Lake
HORN MOUNTAINS
Yellowknife
LABRADOR SEA
Skagway
Juneau
Liard
Great Slave Lake
Fort Resolution
Fort Smith
Nairn
BRITISH COLUMBIA
CARIBOU MOUNTAINS
HUDSON BAY
Churchill
Lake Athabasca
QUEEN CHARLOTTE ISLANDS
Hazelton
COAST MOUNTAINS
ROCKY MOUNTAINS
Peace
CANADA
Reindeer Lake
Goose Bay
NEWFOUNDLAND
Peace River
Churchill
Nelson
Prince Rupert
Prince George
ALBERTA
MANITOBA
Gander
Severn
Fort George
St John's
Edmonton
N. Saskatchewan
SASKATCHEWAN
ONTARIO
Gulf of St. Lawrence
Prince Albert
Lake Winnipegosis
Albany
Fort Albany
PRINCE EDWARD ISLAND
Calgary
Saskatoon
Lake Winnipeg
QUEBEC
NEW BRUNSWICK
Charlottetown
Vancouver Island
Vancouver
Medicine Hat
Lake Manitoba
Regina
Quebec
NOVA SCOTIA
Victoria
S. Saskatchewan
Fredericton
St John
Halifax
PACIFIC OCEAN
Seattle
Winnipeg
Thunder Bay
Lake Superior
Montreal
Duluth
Ottawa
Georgian Bay
UNITED STATES OF AMERICA
Lake Huron
Boston
Missouri
Minneapolis
St Paul
Lake Ontario
Toronto
Mississippi
Lake Michigan
Buffalo
New York
Milwaukee
Detroit
Lake Erie
Cleveland
ATLANTIC OCEAN
A
B
C
D
70°
60°
50°
1
2
3
4
5
6
7
8
9
10
11
12
13
14
15
4
120°
5
110°
6
100°
7
90°
8
80°
9
70°
10
0
500 miles
0
500 kilometres

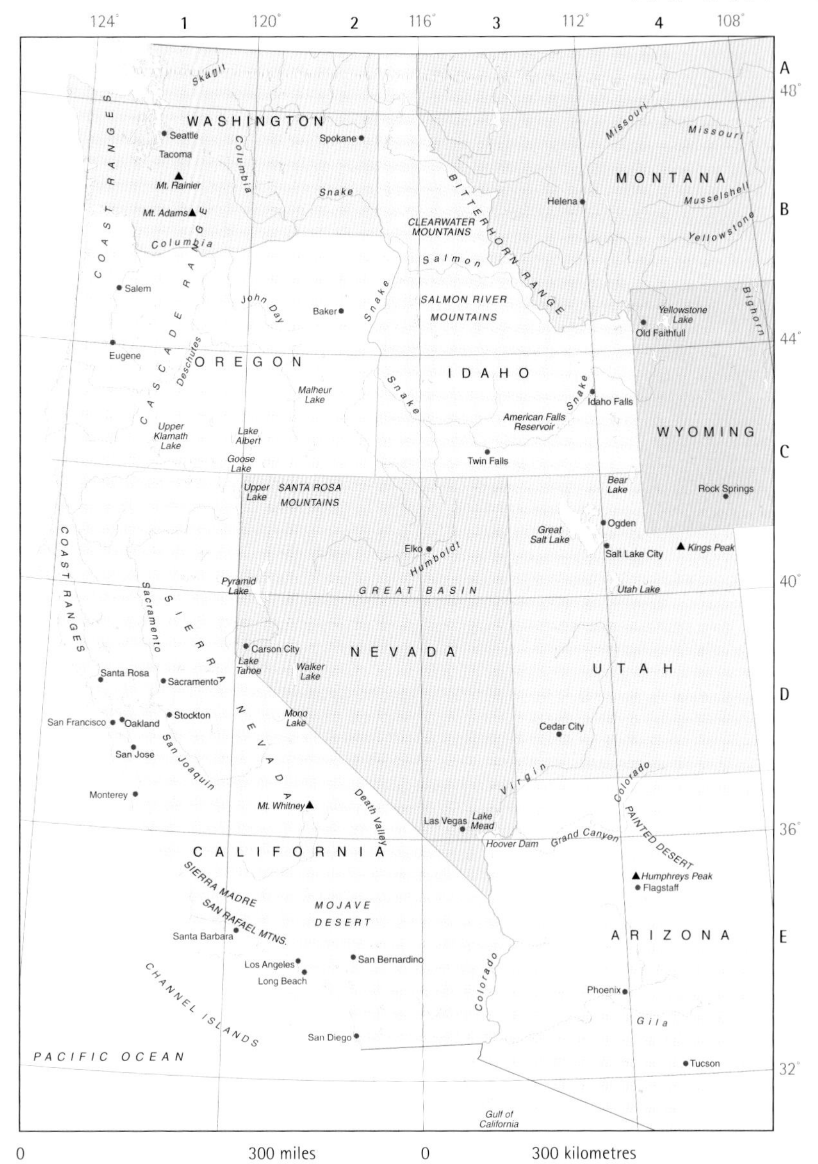
124°
1
120°
2
116°
3
112°
4
108°
A
48°
B
44°
C
40°
D
36°
E
32°
Skagit
COAST RANGES
WASHINGTON
Seattle
Tacoma
Mt. Rainier
Mt. Adams
Columbia
Spokane
Snake
Columbia
CASCADE RANGE
Missouri
Missouri
MONTANA
Helena
Musselshell
Yellowstone
BITTERHORN RANGE
CLEARWATER MOUNTAINS
Salmon
SALMON RIVER MOUNTAINS
Salem
John Day
Baker
Snake
Bighorn
Yellowstone Lake
Old Faithfull
Eugene
Deschutes
OREGON
IDAHO
Snake
Snake
Idaho Falls
Malheur Lake
American Falls Reservoir
Upper Klamath Lake
Lake Albert
Goose Lake
Twin Falls
WYOMING
Upper Lake
SANTA ROSA MOUNTAINS
Bear Lake
Rock Springs
Ogden
Great Salt Lake
Salt Lake City
Kings Peak
Elko
Humboldt
COAST RANGES
Pyramid Lake
GREAT BASIN
Utah Lake
Sacramento
SIERRA NEVADA
Carson City
NEVADA
Lake Tahoe
Walker Lake
UTAH
Santa Rosa
Sacramento
Stockton
San Francisco
Oakland
Mono Lake
Cedar City
San Jose
San Joaquin
Virgin
Colorado
Monterey
Mt. Whitney
Death Valley
PAINTED DESERT
Las Vegas
Lake Mead
Hoover Dam
Grand Canyon
CALIFORNIA
Humphreys Peak
Flagstaff
SIERRA MADRE
SAN RAFAEL MTNS.
MOJAVE DESERT
Santa Barbara
ARIZONA
San Bernardino
Los Angeles
Long Beach
Colorado
CHANNEL ISLANDS
Phoenix
Gila
San Diego
PACIFIC OCEAN
Tucson
Gulf of California
0
300 miles
0
300 kilometres

110° 1 105° 2 100° 3 95° 4 90° 5

A
B
C
D
E

45°
40°
35°
30°

CANADA
Mouse
Red
Lake Sakakawea
Sheyenne
Red Lake
MINNESOTA
Lake Superior
Fort Peck Lake
MONTANA
Yellowstone
NORTH DAKOTA
Fargo
Duluth
Ironwood
MICHIGAN
Mississippi
Missouri
Billings
ROCKY MOUNTAINS
BIGHORN MOUNTAINS
Bighorn
Cody
Gillette
Sundance
Cheyenne
James
Minneapolis
Minnesota
WISCONSIN
La Crosse
SOUTH DAKOTA
Sioux Falls
Milwaukee
Madison
WYOMING
Cedar
LARAMIE RANGE
Sioux City
Fort Dodge
Chicago
NEBRASKA
IOWA
Rock Springs
Davenport
Des Moines
Laramie
Omaha
Cheyenne
North Platte
Illinois
Lincoln
Fort Collins
Platte
COLORADO
St Joseph
ILLINOIS
Denver
Mt. Egbert
Kansas City
St Louis
Mt. Harvard
Pikes Peak
Colorado Springs
Hays
Salina
SANGRE DE CRISTO MOUNTAINS
Mt. Wilson
Arkansas
KANSAS
MISSOURI
Lamar
Dodge City
Wichita
Springfield
San Juan
CIMARRON
Rio Grande
Tulsa
Santa Fe
Oklahoma City
Arkansas
Las Vegas
Canadian
Memphis
Amarillo
Little Rock
Hot Springs
NEW MEXICO
OKLAHOMA
ARKANSAS
Columbus
Lubbock
Wichita Falls
Roswell
El Dorado
MISSISSIPPI
SACRAMENTO MOUNTAINS
Fort Worth
Dallas
TEXAS
LOUISIANA
El Paso
Trinity
Sabine
Natchez
Pecos
Rio Grande
Leon
Brazos
EDWARDS PLATEAU
Baton Rouge
New Orleans
Colorado
Houston
Port Arthur
Del Rio
Galveston
San Antonio
Laredo
Corpus Christi
GULF OF MEXICO
MEXICO
Brownsville

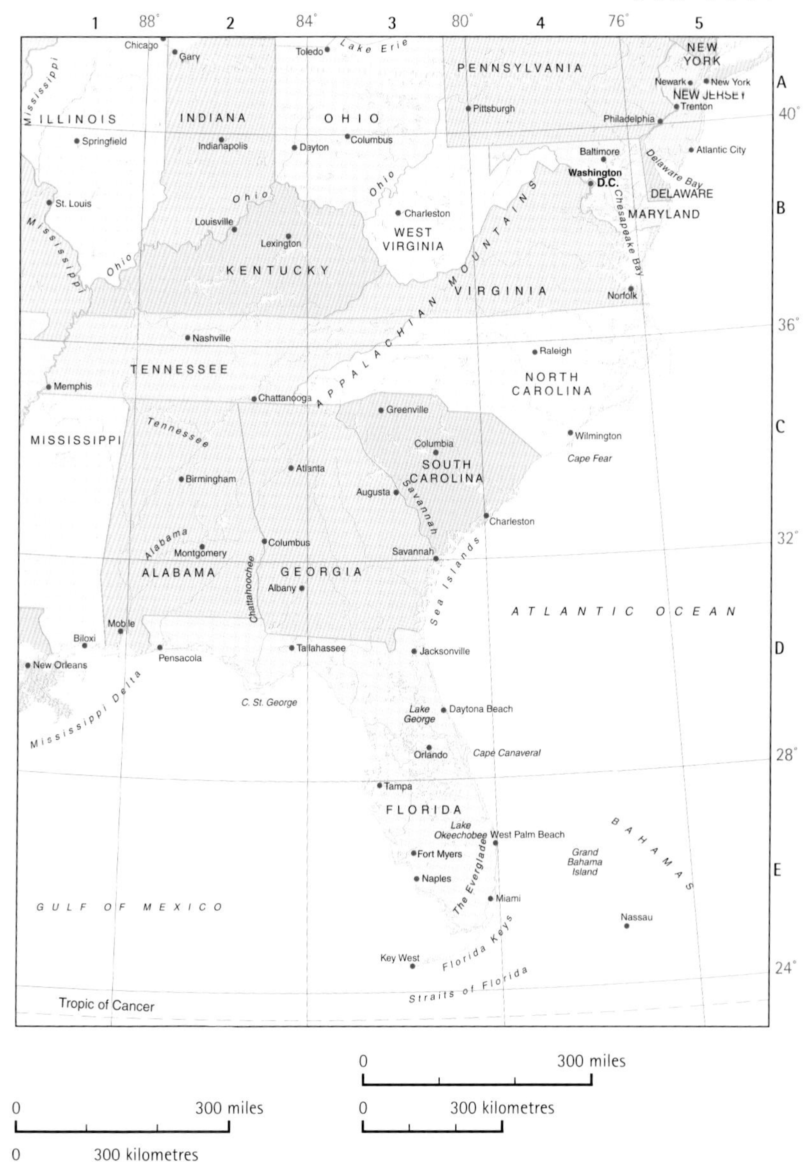
1
88°
2
84°
3
80°
4
76°
5
A
B
C
D
E
40°
36°
32°
28°
24°
Chicago
Gary
Toledo
Lake Erie
PENNSYLVANIA
NEW YORK
Newark
New York
NEW JERSEY
Trenton
Mississippi
ILLINOIS
INDIANA
OHIO
Pittsburgh
Philadelphia
Springfield
Indianapolis
Dayton
Columbus
Baltimore
Atlantic City
Delaware Bay
Washington D.C.
DELAWARE
Ohio
St. Louis
Charleston
MARYLAND
Chesapeake Bay
Louisville
Lexington
WEST VIRGINIA
KENTUCKY
APPALACHIAN MOUNTAINS
VIRGINIA
Norfolk
Nashville
Raleigh
TENNESSEE
NORTH CAROLINA
Memphis
Chattanooga
Greenville
Tennessee
MISSISSIPPI
Wilmington
Columbia
Cape Fear
SOUTH CAROLINA
Atlanta
Birmingham
Augusta
Savannah
Charleston
Alabama
Columbus
Montgomery
Savannah
ALABAMA
GEORGIA
Chattahoochee
Albany
Sea Islands
ATLANTIC OCEAN
Mobile
Biloxi
Pensacola
Tallahassee
Jacksonville
New Orleans
Mississippi Delta
C. St. George
Lake George
Daytona Beach
Orlando
Cape Canaveral
Tampa
FLORIDA
BAHAMAS
Lake Okeechobee
West Palm Beach
Grand Bahama Island
Fort Myers
Naples
The Everglades
GULF OF MEXICO
Miami
Nassau
Key West
Florida Keys
Straits of Florida
Tropic of Cancer
0
300 miles
0
300 kilometres
0
300 miles
0
300 kilometres

1 110° 2 100° 3 90°

A

B

C

D

30°

20°

10°

Colorado
Canadian
White
UNITED STATES OF AMER
San Diego
Phoenix
Red
Mississipp
Tilauana
Dallas
El Paso
Ciudad Juárez
Brazos
Pecos
Baja California
Gulf of California
New
I. de Cedros
Hermosillo
SIERRA MADRE OCCIDENT
Rio Grande
Houston
San Antonio
Punta Eugenie
Chihuahua
SIERRA MADRE ORIENTAL
MEXICO
Monterrey
Matamoros
GULF O
La Paz
Durango
Cabo Falso
Tampico
León
Guadalajara
Cabo Corrientes
Bahia de Campeche
Campeche
L. de Chapala
Naucalpan
Mexico City
Veracruz
Laguna de Terminos
Manzanillo
Puebla
Coatzacoalcas
Balsas
Oaxaca
Acapulco
Golfo de Tehuantapec
GUATE
Guatemala
PACIFIC OCEAN
San Salv
EL SAL

4
80°
5
70°
6
60°
Bermuda
ATLANTIC OCEAN
Tropic of Cancer
Tampa
BAHAMAS IS.
BAHAMA ISLANDS
Miami
Nassau
Andros I.
TURKS & CAICOS ISLANDS
XICO
Havana
CUBA
Camagüey
Great Inagua
DOMINICAN REPUBLIC
San Juan
VIRGIN Is.
Barbuda
Antigua
Montserrat
Guadeloupe
St. Kitts & Nevis
PUERTO RICO
HAITI
Santo Domingo
Port-au-Prince
Isla de la Juventad
Yucatan Channel
GREATER ANTILLES
Dominica
Martinique
St. Lucia
Barbados
St. Vincent
CAYMAN IS.
CAYMAN ISLANDS
Jamaica
Kingston
JAMAICA
Grenada
Tobago
Trinidad
LESSER ANTILLES
elize City
nopan
ZE
of Honduras
HONDURAS
CARIBBEAN SEA
Netherlands Antilles
cigalpa
Maracaibo
Barranquilla
Orinoco
Caroni
NICARAGUA
nagua
Lago de Nicaragua
Apure
VENEZUELA
San Jose
Golfo de los Mosquitos
Panama
San Christóbal
COSTA RICA
PANAMA
Gulf of Panama
Cauca
Magdalena
COLOMBIA
Medellín
Meta
Bogotá
Guaviare
Uraricuer
Branco
BRAZIL
0
500 miles
0
500 kilometres

CARIBBEAN SEA
Gulf of Venezuela
Barranquilla
Caracas
Port of Spain
TRINIDAD & TOBAGO
PANAMA
Lake Maracaibo
ATLANTIC OCEAN
Gulf of Panama
Orinoco
VENEZUELA
Georgetown
Paramaribo
Medellín
GUYANA
FRENCH GUIANA
Bogotá
Cayenne
Cali
Magdalena
SURINAM
COLOMBIA
GUIANA HIGHLANDS
Orinoco
Huila
Macapá
Quito
Negro
Chimborazo
Japurá
Amazona
ECUADOR
Putumayo
Manaus
Tocantins
São Luis
Marañon
Xingu
Juruá
Madeira
ANDES MOUNTAINS
Purus
Araguaia
Parnaíba
Recife
Nevado Huascarán
Maceió
BRAZIL
SIERRA DOS PARECIS
PERU
Lima
Salvador
PLANALTO DE MATO GROSSO
Lake Titicaca
CAMPOS
Nevado Ancohuma
BRAZILIAN HIGHLANDS
Brasília
La Paz
BOLIVIA
Lake Poopó
CHACO
PACIFIC OCEAN
Belo Horizone
A
B
C
D
10°
0°
10°
20°

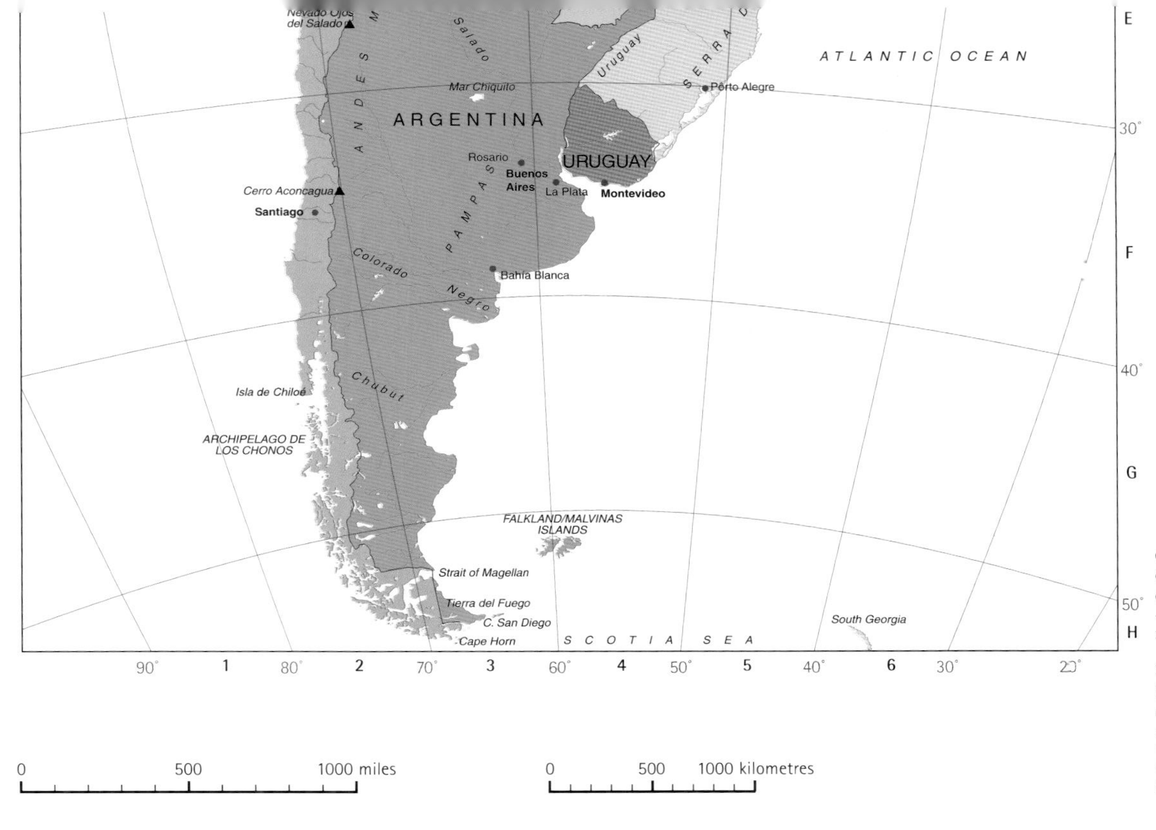
ATLANTIC OCEAN
SCOTIA SEA
ARGENTINA
URUGUAY
Nevado Ojos del Salado
Salado
Uruguay
Pôrto Alegre
Mar Chiquito
Rosario
Buenos Aires
La Plata
Montevideo
Cerro Aconcagua
Santiago
PAMPAS
ANDES
Colorado
Bahía Blanca
Negro
Chubut
Isla de Chiloé
ARCHIPELAGO DE LOS CHONOS
FALKLAND/MALVINAS ISLANDS
Strait of Magellan
Tierra del Fuego
C. San Diego
Cape Horn
South Georgia
E
F
G
H
1
2
3
4
5
6
90°
80°
70°
60°
50°
40°
30°
20°
0
500
1000 miles
0
500
1000 kilometres

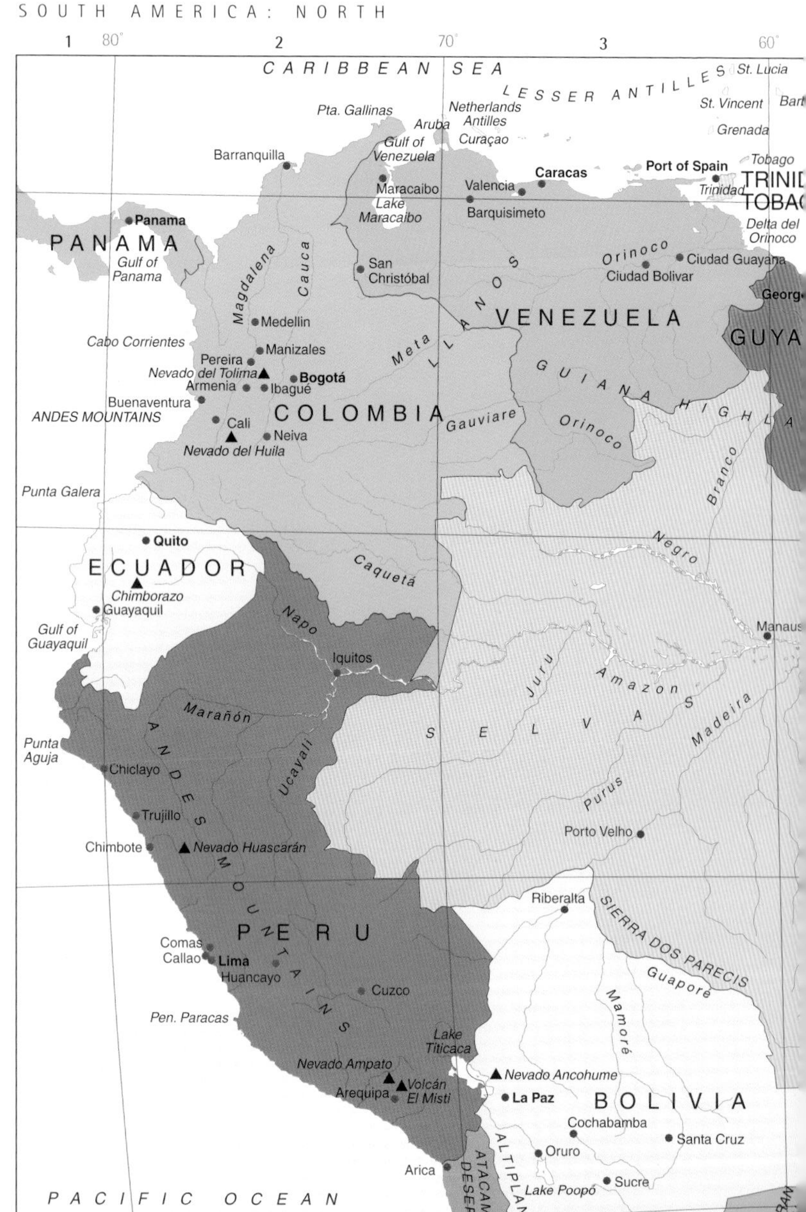
1
80°
2
70°
3
60°
CARIBBEAN SEA
LESSER ANTILLES
St. Lucia
St. Vincent
Grenada
Tobago
Trinidad
Pta. Gallinas
Netherlands Antilles
Aruba
Curaçao
Gulf of Venezuela
Barranquilla
Maracaibo
Lake Maracaibo
Valencia
Caracas
Port of Spain
Barquisimeto
Delta del Orinoco
Panama
PANAMA
Gulf of Panama
Magdalena
Cauca
San Christóbal
LLANOS
Orinoco
Ciudad Bolivar
Ciudad Guayana
VENEZUELA
Medellin
Cabo Corrientes
Manizales
Pereira
Meta
Nevado del Tolima
Bogotá
Armenia
Ibagué
GUIANA HIGHLANDS
Buenaventura
ANDES MOUNTAINS
Cali
COLOMBIA
Gauviare
Orinoco
Neiva
Nevado del Huila
Branco
Punta Galera
Negro
Quito
ECUADOR
Caquetá
Chimborazo
Guayaquil
Napo
Gulf of Guayaquil
Manaus
Iquitos
Juru
Amazon
Marañón
SELVAS
Madeira
Punta Aguja
ANDES MOUNTAINS
Ucayali
Chiclayo
Purus
Trujillo
Porto Velho
Chimbote
Nevado Huascarán
Riberalta
SIERRA DOS PARECIS
PERU
Comas
Callao
Lima
Huancayo
Guaporé
Mamoré
Cuzco
Pen. Paracas
Lake Titicaca
Nevado Ampato
Nevado Ancohume
Volcán El Misti
Arequipa
La Paz
BOLIVIA
Cochabamba
Santa Cruz
ALTIPLANO
Oruro
Arica
PACIFIC OCEAN
Lake Poopó
Sucre

4
50°
5
40°
6
0
5000 miles
0
5000 kilometres
A
10°
Paramaribo
FRENCH GUIANA
Cayenne
RINAM
ATLANTIC OCEAN
B
Macapá
0°
B. de Marajó
I. de Marajó
Belém
Amazon
B. de
São Marcos
São Luis
Tocantins
Fortalez
Teresina
Xingu
Ponta do
Calcanhar
C
Natal
R A Z I L
Joao
Pessoa
CAATINGAS
Araguaia
Parnaíba
São Francisco
Recife
Juazeiro
Maceió
10°
Barragem de
Sobradinho
Paranatinga
Aracaju
Salvador
Carinhanha
D
Cuiabá
BRAZILIAN
PLANALTO DE
Brasília
MATO GROSSO
Goiânia
HIGHLANDS
Montes Claros
CAMPOS
Paraná
Belo Horizonte
Campo Grande

A
B
C
20°
30°
Arica
Lake Poopó
Sucre
ALTIPLANO
ATACAMA DESERT
BOLIVIA
GRAN CHACO
PLANALTO DE
MATO GROSSO
BRAZILIAN HIGHLANDS
Caravelas
Paraná
Grande
Doce
Campo Grande
Belo Horizonte
Tietê
BRAZIL
Represa Ilha Grande
Paranapanema
Concepción
Rio de Janeiro
PARAGUAY
Cabo Frio
São Paulo
Santos
Tropic of Capricorn
Antofagasta
Pilcomayo
Volcán Llullaillaco
Bermejo
Asunción
Itaipu Res.
SERRA DO MAR
Curitiba
Rio Iguaçu
Formosa
Paraguay
San Miguel de Tucumán
Nevado Ojos del Salado
Corrientes
Uruguai
Florianópolis
Copiapó
Salado
Laguna
Cabo Sta. Marta Grande
SIERRA DE CORDOBA
Paran
Santa Maria
Pôrto Alegre
Coquimbo
Mar Chiquito
Cordoba
Concordia
Tacuarembo
Pelotas
Lagôa dos Patos
San Juan
Rio Grande
Lagôa Mirim
Santa Fe
Paraná
Cerro Aconcagua
Mendoza
Rosario
Negro
Valparaiso
URUGUAY
Santiago
PAMPAS
Buenos Aires
Montevideo
ATLANTIC OCEAN
Salado
La Plata
Rio de La Plata
San Rafael
Pta. Norte
C. Carranza
Cabo San Antonio
ARGENTINA
Chillán
Mar del Plata
Concepción
Cabo Corrientes
Bahia Blanca
Colorado
Bahia Blanca
CHILE
Negro

Peninsula Valdés
Rawson
Isla de Chiloé
Chubut
C. Quilán
ARCHIPELAGO DE LOS CHONOS
Comodoro Rivadavia
Golfo de San Jorge
D
Lago Buenos Aires
C. Tres Puntas
Deseado
Puerto
Golfo de Penas
Chico
Isla Wellington
Puerto Santa Cruz
FALKLAND/MALVINAS ISLANDS
Bahia Grande
West Falkland
Stanley
East Falkland
50°
Río Gallegos
ARCHIPELAGO REINA ADELAIDE
Strait of Magellan
Punta Arenas
Tierra del Fuego
C. San Diego
Isla Santa Inés
E
SCOTIA SEA
South Georgia
Drake Passage
Cape Horn
80°
1
70°
2
60°
3
50°
4
40°
5
30°
0
500 miles
0
500 kilometres

Index